MW01503401

Data Processing Systems
Analysis and Design

Data Processing Systems Analysis and Design

Robert J. Condon
Westchester Community College
Valhalla, New York

RESTON PUBLISHING COMPANY, INC.
Reston, Virginia 22090
A Prentice-Hall Company

Library of Congress Cataloging in Publication Data

Condon, Robert J   1934-
    Data processing systems analysis and design.

    1. Electronic data processing—Business.   2. Sys-
tem analysis.   I. Title.
HF5548.2.C615   658′.05′4   74-11195
ISBN 0-87909-176-2

© 1975 by
Reston Publishing Company, Inc.
A Prentice-Hall Company
Box 547
Reston, Virginia 22090

10 9 8 7 6 5 4 3 2 1

Printed in the United States of America.

To Margaret and Mae Condon

Contents

Preface

This text is designed specifically for the college student who has had an introductory course in data processing or computer technology and is now taking his first course in systems analysis. In it we discuss how a company organizes itself to use data processing equipment more effectively, and teach the use of the various tools employed by the systems analyst in the creation of better systems. The text, which is divided into five parts, is designed to teach the student what the systems development cycle is and how to use systems tools in each phase of the cycle.

Part 1 explains the use of data processing systems in today's business environment and defines the roles played by people in an organization in planning, designing, testing, and implementing a new system.

Part 2 introduces elementary systems techniques and tools. The use of computer hardware, charting, operations research, and forms design are explained on a very fundamental level. At this stage the reader should have a working knowledge of the basic systems tools, so that he will understand their practical use in subsequent parts.

The third part explains in detail the key steps in the systems development cycle: feasibility study, systems design, and testing and conversion. Related techniques are interspersed so that the student may learn the technique at the particular stage of systems development when it is used most frequently. Data gathering is discussed with feasibility studies; systems documentation is associated with systems design and with testing and conversion.

The final two parts deal with some of the practical applications and considerations in systems analysis: direct access techniques, data and project control, and systems management.

Effective computer systems require an understanding of the interrelationship of each phase of systems development and a mastery of the systems analyst's tools. More importantly, they require a realization that systems are carried out by people—and understanding people, their working habits and their needs, is the greatest asset that a systems analyst can possess.

Robert J. Condon

part I

Systems Analysis
in Business

chapter **1**

Systems Development

Objectives

You will learn the ways in which the term "system" is used today in business applications. Since businesses constantly change, we shall discuss the steps that a business takes to install a new system to meet its changing requirements.

From the time that a request for a systems change is made until the time when the new system is in operation, an organization must plan, design, test, control, and implement the proposed system.

For a system to work properly, management must set the goals and provide the means for achieving these goals. The data processing department must design and program the system, and then test it. The operations department must run the new system when it is ready, and check it constantly to see that it is performing properly.

2

WHAT IS A SYSTEM?

Many people use the term "system" freely, often with no precise definition in mind. One hears: "What we need around here is a new system" or "This system isn't really working." The "system" is blamed for a wide range of business problems, and, as you will learn, a firm's effectiveness is largely dependent upon its data processing systems.

We may define a system informally as a set of procedures designed to accomplish a predetermined objective. Although the term "systems" is used in many other fields, we are concerned only with business systems.

A business system (Fig. 1-1) usually has the following characteristics:

1. Systems objectives are defined by corporate management.
2. The system is composed of procedural steps.
3. The system uses equipment.
4. The system produces information.
5. The system is controlled to ensure accuracy of information.

TYPES OF SYSTEMS

Although most complex systems now use computers to achieve their objectives, many developed from manual and accounting machine systems. Most companies once used, and many small companies still do use, manual systems for their accounting records. Such systems are appropriate where the volume of transactions is relatively low. Larger companies have gradually converted their manual systems to accounting machine systems. This movement began soon after World War II, when business became more aware of the potential of the punched card for the solution of paperwork problems. Accounting machines are adequate for the data processing needs of many businesses, but as a firm grows and its business problems become more complex, it reaches a point when it requires computer systems.

Each type of system—manual, accounting machine, and computer—developed techniques to efficiently produce accurate results. Each borrowed principles from the system that preceded it, yet each required an entirely new approach to corporate problem solving. Moreover, as the computer developed, each successive technical breakthrough required new knowledge, new techniques, and a new corporate awareness. As a result, many levels of systems sophistication exist today.

Besides being categorized by type of equipment, systems can be

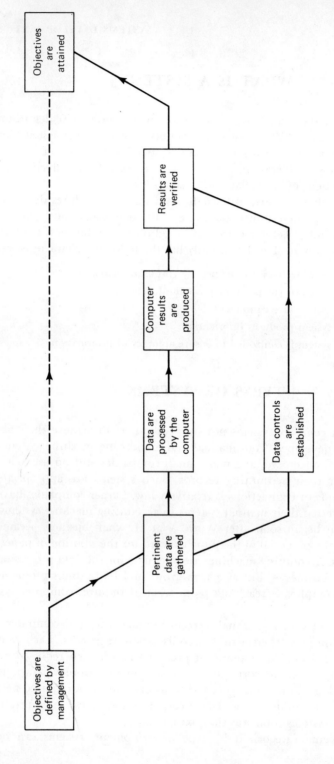

Fig. 1-1 Components of a computer-based system.

4

defined by their purpose. Some systems merely keep records; they gather data, process, store, and make reports from them. Most payroll systems fall into this classification. Data are gathered from time cards or clerical records; paychecks are produced, and salary information is stored to produce quarterly and annual reports for tax purposes. A management information system (MIS) would do all of this and in addition would select and summarize information for management's use. In a payroll system, for example, an MIS might provide data for analyzing personnel turnover or evaluating the recruiting program of the company. Many corporations today find it difficult to advance beyond the record-keeping level of sophistication, either because they do not have the systems knowledge required, or because their management is not aware of the potential of existing computer systems.

Systems analysis began in the 1940s, when companies applied assembly-line efficiencies to clerical problems. Computers were being developed at that time, but independently. Business first saw the potential usefulness of the computer for the solution of accounting and mathematical problems. As its possible uses became clearer, it was apparent that the computer could fulfill the information requirements of an entire business organization (Fig. 1-2). Thus the "integrated" or "total" system was developed. The total system coordinates the gathering and use of all the data within an organization. The company is, in effect, organized around the computer. All the information coming into the company is channeled through the computer. All reports and management information are obtained from the computer. The company's activities, including product development, billing, sales analysis, and inventory, are interrelated because each is tied into a common computer system. Life insurance is a good example of an industry that uses a total system.

The major functions of an insurance company are:

1. Developing new types of insurance coverage
2. Selling policies
3. Underwriting (risk evaluation)
4. Policy issuance
5. Maintaining accurate records
6. Paying insurance benefits

The master file which contains the essential data for each policy, is the basis for integrating these functions. Records of premium payment are maintained accurately on the master file. When benefits are to be paid, a computer program can analyze and print the various options that the beneficiaries are entitled to. Applications for insurance are evaluated by an underwriting program, and when the application is accepted, the

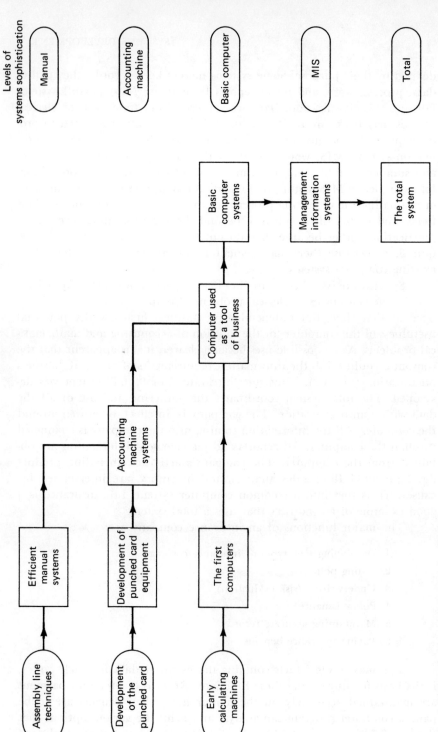

Fig. 1-2 How computer systems developed.

6

contract is written and the initial premium is recorded by computer. Sales data, such as individual salesman's performance, are continually analyzed through the computer system. The system, moreover, analyzes the types of policies that are selling well and points out potential combinations of benefits that would appeal to the company's customers. Thus in a total system, the computer integrates a company's major functions.

A system includes the following components (Fig. 1-3):

procedures—both clerical and computer

programs—for the storage and retrieval of information and the general operation of the computer

hardware—all data processing equipment

personnel—professionals and other users of the equipment and procedures

files—the organization's data base

MINI-CASE 1.1

Two years ago, Larry Mahoney started designing, manufacturing, and selling men's ties. His little business has done well; he now sells his ties through three local retail stores. Last week, Larry went to the bank to obtain a loan for expanding the business. Larry's plans include:

Purchasing sewing, dyeing, and cutting equipment

Renting a small area for manufacturing his ties

Hiring 12 people: 10 in production, a full-time salesman, and an assistant to supervise the workers, arrange distribution of the ties through over 50 retail outlets, and coordinate the purchase of raw material.

The bank liked Larry's expansion plans and were very impressed with him as a designer and enterprising businessman. However, the bank said that it would not advance him the money until he presented a plan of the systems he would use in his operation.

Larry has called you to help him formulate a plan to organize the new company. Specifically, he needs help in the following areas:

1. What type of information will Mr. Mahoney require to manage his business effectively?

2. Which aspects of his business will need written procedures?

3. What systems objectives would his business have?

4. What types of controls are required in this type of business?

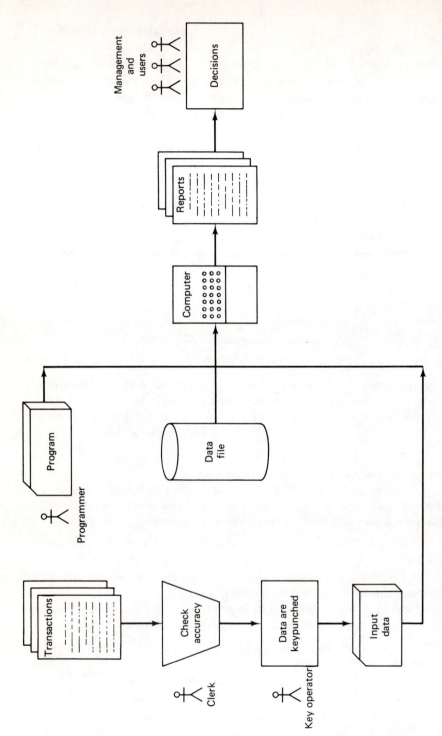

Fig. 1-3 Typical computer system.

8

STEPS IN THE SYSTEMS DEVELOPMENT CYCLE

Some organizations have rigid policies and procedures for completing each step in the development of a new system or the improvement of existing systems. In other organizations, usually smaller ones, this development is an informal process, often directed by an individual who devotes only part of his time to it. Most organizations use both formal and informal methods to bring about change. Regardless of the approach, the following steps are taken wherever systems exist:

1. Systems requests
2. Selection and authorization of systems studies
3. Feasibility studies
4. Systems design
   a. Data gathering and analysis
   b. Systems specification
   c. Program writing
5. Testing and conversion
6. Systems operation

Systems Requests: Origination

A company president says to his controller, "When am I going to get some up-to-date information on our cash flow?" A payroll clerk asks a computer programmer, "Couldn't we possibly combine the overtime check with the normal salary check?" A young management trainee writes a memo to the manager of the systems department outlining his thoughts on the information needs of his department. All of these are systems requests, yet each will be handled in a different way.

Selection and Authorization of Systems Studies

Organizations require some mechanism to review requests for new or revised systems. Ideally, an organization forms a selection committee of representatives from several operating areas in the company, as well as spokesmen for top management and data processing. This group should be both senior and representative enough to provide an objective review for all requests presented to it. The selection committee screens requests for general feasibility and then rejects them as impractical, tables them for consideration at a more appropriate date, or approves a more detailed look at the request, called a feasibility study (Fig. 1-4).

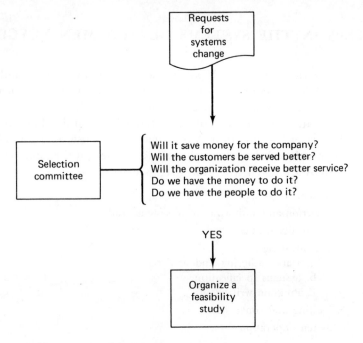

Fig. 1-4 Task of the selection committee.

In smaller companies, the work of the selection committee may be done by an individual, perhaps the data processing manager, who has the knowledge and authority to screen the organization's systems requests.

Most requests cannot receive equal consideration. The decision-making process within an organization is the product of both the formal and informal corporate structure, and the stronger voices in an organization will be heard by the group that is evaluating requests. However, other, more objective criteria exist for the selection of systems projects.

The two primary restrictions on undertaking systems studies are limited financial and human resources. A corporation usually has a fixed amount in its budget for systems studies and only those studies that indicate a reasonable cost saving, an improved customer service, or more efficient internal organization can be considered. Few companies have sufficient funds to investigate all the studies that may have merit, so the selection committee must approve only those projects which are most beneficial to the entire organization.

The best way to do this is for the selection committee to analyze each request on the basis of estimated cost versus potential benefit. Since the request may be in rough form when it is considered by the selection committee, the committee must have sufficient knowledge concerning the nature of the request and considerable insight into the needs of the corporation. It must also possess a working knowledge of computer potential and systems cost.

Limited human resources is a great deterrent in undertaking systems studies because the people in a systems department have a limited amount of skill and time, and these must be concentrated where they are most effective. Their efforts cannot be squandered in projects that do not justify their costs.

The Feasibility Study

Once the selection committee has approved a request, it directs the systems department, in writing, to initiate a feasibility study. The details of conducting a feasibility study will be discussed in Chapter 6; here we will merely point out the relationship of the feasibility study to the overall systems development cycle. A feasibility study determines the best way to achieve the objective of the systems request and is a preliminary step to the design of a system. In the process of its investigation, the individual or group who conducts the study often uncovers alternative methods of achieving those objectives and should point them out for management's consideration. Ultimately, the feasibility team determines a general solution to the problem and states its plan for implementing its solution in a formal feasibility report.

A feasibility study is really a systems study done on a small scale. It requires virtually all the steps necessary to design a system, but the steps are not done in full detail. In effect, the feasibility group investigates a suggestion or problem in some detail, finds a feasible solution (or perhaps finds the idea not feasible at all), and presents its findings to management. When management approves the plan of the feasibility team, a new system is designed.

Designing the New System

Systems design is a complicated, precise process that coordinates the efforts of many people, including systems professionals and knowledgeable people from the user areas. Usually, a system is designed by a project team, consisting of a project leader and his staff of systems analysts, programmers, and specialists from the user areas. Smaller systems may be handled by an individual working in cooperation with the systems users. Systems design will always include the gathering and analysis of data, systems specifications, and the actual designing and writing of the programs.

data gathering

To be effective, systems analysts must gather both facts and opinions pertaining to a problem. Such data must be gathered from every source in the organization. Company reports and memoranda should be studied, and employees should be interviewed at every level of the organization. The optimal solution will depend largely on the quality of these data.

data analysis

After facts and opinions are gathered, they must be organized so that meaningful conclusions may be drawn from them. Systems analysts never create entirely new systems: they blend ideas until they come up with a combination that can achieve management's objectives. The key to systems analysis is to evaluate ideas and opinions and synthesize them into an effective system.

Many techniques have been developed to assist the systems analyst analyze data. For example, PERT charts are used to lay out complicated scheduling problems; systems flowcharts graphically describe an overall system to management and other systems professionals; and block diagrams and decision tables document the progammed solution to a problem.

new systems specification

When the data have been collected and analyzed, the systems design team presents its solutions to the users. This presentation is more detailed than the feasibility study and is designed to educate user personnel. At this stage the system has been designed in reasonable detail and the users should be able to evaluate its impact. We must emphasize that the formal specification of a system must be complemented with frequent and informal exchanges of ideas between the systems designers and the systems users.

The systems specification normally contains the following elements:

1. A design of the master files (data base) from which the organization will retrieve required information

2. A list of the programs needed to meet the systems objectives

3. A schedule of target dates for implementing the new system

4. An estimate of the impact of the new system upon the user areas, other existing systems, and the total organization

5. Samples of input and output to be used in the new system

When the specification is presented, the systems design team is reasonably sure that its system will be workable. Of course, the systems design team will encounter many difficulties as it produces each program and attempts to coordinate the various portions of the system. The systems specification is the blueprint which can help avoid major breakdowns in communication, which could lead to serious problems in the conversion to a new system.

In complex systems, a systems specification may be presented several times as the design evolves in deeper detail. Everyone involved is kept well informed, and the final design should surprise no one.

detailed systems design

Systems planners too often begin the actual detailed design of a system without spending enough effort on the planning steps discussed above. This often results in a beautiful system which, unfortunately, does not solve the problems of the company.

In the systems design phase, every detail of the proposed system must be plotted and its relationship with every other phase of the project examined. The various files must be correlated into a data base that is complete, has no redundancies, and provides information accurately and efficiently. The input documents and the output reports must be completely designed. Finally, all programs must be outlined to determine whether or not the input to the system will result in the expected output.

program writing

Program writing comes rather late in the systems development cycle. When the project is large enough, a programmer might only write a portion of a program and then coordinate his portion (or module) with at least one other program. Program writing should not begin until the input, output, program requirements, and the relationship among the various programs are established.

Testing and Conversion

No system works perfectly the first time it is tried. One measurement of a systems analyst's effectiveness is his ability to test a system. The following are the basic elements of a systems test:

    1. Testing each program individually.

    2. Testing the interrelationship of each program to the entire system.

    3. Testing the system and all its programs with "test data." Test data

are designed specifically to try out each condition the system is expected to handle.

4. Testing the system with "live data." Live data are the actual data that will be used in the system. This type of test will indicate that the system handles each type of transaction correctly, but also that it can handle the volume of transactions anticipated.

The process of systems conversion is a touchy one. Careful planning is necessary to implement the new system without disrupting service to the users or the customers. Conversion strategies are examined in Chapter 9.

The New System in Operation

Eventually the old system has been converted to the new and is operating satisfactorily. Normally, new systems have many minor problems that the systems department and the user areas must clear up before the system runs smoothly. Carefully prepared systems can be "debugged" without causing total systems failure. Shortcuts in design and analysis do, however, increase the risk of failure.

The Life Cycle of a System

Systems, like all living things, must change and adapt to survive. Eventually, the corporate president will say to his controller, "Our cash-flow reports do not accurately reflect our short-term paper. Isn't there anything you can do about it?"

The better the planning, the longer the systems operation phase will be, yet with rapid changes in business today, we must think of systems development as an on-going process (Fig. 1-5) and learn to think of a system as having a temporary existence.

ROLES IN SYSTEMS DEVELOPMENT

Many areas within an organization must perform well for a system to satisfy corporate needs. When the systems department has sole responsibility for developing new systems, unsatisfactory results are predictable. Developing even a very small system involves at least one user area, the systems group, programmers, and most importantly, management. For it to be successful, each of these areas must be included in the systems development.

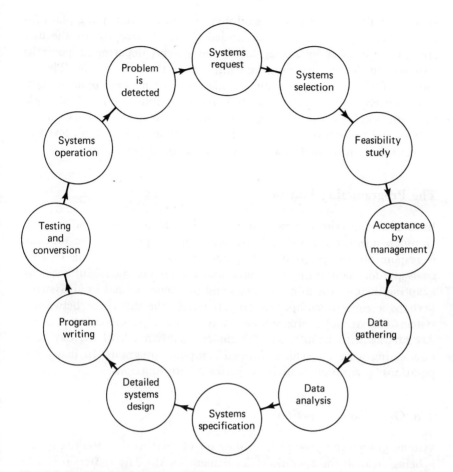

Fig. 1-5 Systems development cycle.

In any systems effort, management has the most important responsibilities. Management must set appropriate goals and must provide the systems group with the tools to achieve those goals. This includes providing financial and human resources, and, more importantly, providing an environment in which change is acceptable to the user areas of the company. Management must set up the mechanism through which the organization can change itself.

The Systems Department

A systems department conducts studies to design and implement new systems. It also participates in feasibility studies, recommending plans for effecting change. When a recommended change is accepted by the user area and approved by management, the systems department pools its resources to design, program, and implement the new system. The resources of a systems department include such systems development skills as a knowledge of computer potential and limitations; the knack of working with people; a knowledge of the company, its goals, and its current systems and procedures and the ability to communicate with all levels of the organization through oral, written, and graphic persuasion.

The Programming Function

In some organizations, programming is a part of systems; in others, it is an independent, but closely related function. The programming function is responsible for preparing computer programs to meet the system's goals and for maintaining these programs throughout the life of a system, adapting them to the minor changes and problems normal in all systems. Perhaps a gross oversimplification can clarify the difference between a systems analyst and a programmer. A systems analyst spends most of his day talking with people; a programmer spends much of his day communicating with a machine through computer programs. In many corporations "programmer–analysts" perform both functions.

The Operations Function

Systems groups and programmers do most of their work while the system is being created; the operations department (or the data center) performs the day-to-day operations of the system after it has been developed. The data center, working from procedures and instructions provided by the systems and programming areas, operates the equipment and monitors the system to keep it as error-free as possible, and to make certain that the system actually performs as expected.

The Control Function

Every system has controls to assure up-to-date and accurate output. Chapter 12 discusses data control methods.

Responsibility for data control is usually distributed among many parts of an organization. Programmers write routines in their programs to check the accuracy of input data. Control clerks compare computer output with predetermined totals before distributing reports. Users spot-check computer-produced reports before basing decisions on them. The systems department, during the design phase, must establish control points through which operating personnel can continually check the system.

The User Areas

Although they are discussed last, the users of the computer's data are very important. The computer system is made for them, and they alone are the judges of the system's effectiveness. Systems must satisfy the users, whether the user be a billing department, the company's customers, or corporate management.

MINI-CASE 1.2

Double Duty Copying Company manufactures duplicating and printing equipment. Starting with a small factory in a Philadelphia suburb, Double Duty now has six manufacturing locations on the East Coast. Some plants turn out large printing presses and offset reproducers; others specialize in office copiers. Although Double Duty is not one of the "Big Three" in its industry, it has a rapidly expanding market throughout the United States and Western Europe.

Until now, Fred O'Connor, the company president, has remained steadfast in his opposition to installing electronic data processing equipment. Two years ago, a computer manufacturer was invited to make a study of Double Duty's data processing needs. Its recommendation to install a third-generation computer was rejected by Mr. O'Connor. In a sharply worded memo, Mr. O'Connor outlined his reasons for not installing a computer at that time. These arguments included the following points:

1. The company has done very well up to this point without a computer.

2. Double Duty is a manufacturing and marketing organization. It does not have the technical expertise for installing a computer.

3. The computer manufacturer's recommendations indicated that it would take 4 years before the computer would begin to save money. Mr. O'Connor feels that he could increase the sales force by 25 percent for the money to install a computer.

During the past 2 years the company has continued to prosper under Mr. O'Connor. Four more copiers have been added to the product line and total sales have increased 40 percent during this period. Business is so good that Double Duty is beginning to have some trouble keeping up with orders. Sales projections for the next 5 years indicate an annual growth of 15 percent per year. The number of employees, 500 just 2 years ago, is approaching 800 and will exceed 1,400 in 5 years.

You are the corporate controller and a very good friend of Mr. O'Connor. You have given some thought to the possibility of installing computer equipment. In a brief summary, state for Mr. O'Connor the criteria upon which you think he should base his decision concerning a future computer installation. Include in your summary some suggestions as to what Mr. O'Connor should do to be in a better position to evaluate recommendations on computer installations.

SAMPLE SOLUTION TO MINI-CASE 1.2

TO: Fred O'Connor
FROM:
DATE: June 27, 19--
RE: Organizing for Computer Analysis

Recent developments in our organization, specifically rising payroll costs and the inability to handle orders properly, have created the need to investigate again the possibility of installing a computer. Although our sales are up 40 percent over the past 2 years, our staff has increased by 60 percent. We are losing much potential profit in what is becoming excessive clerical and production costs.

As of the moment, we are not in a position to properly evaluate our EDP requirements. We must develop data processing expertise within the organization and not be entirely dependent upon outsiders for advice. I propose establishing a committee of managers and staff members to review data processing needs and begin to develop the necessary expertise. This group could have outside professional help such as consultants and computer manufacturer representatives available to it as we develop and acquire the necessary internal expertise.

In the past we evaluated the possibiilty of installing a computer largely on the potential savings it would bring. I suggest that the proposed committee establish the following criteria for evaluating potential data processing systems:

1. Does the company have the necessary financial resources for the undertaking?

2. What management and technical expertise will be required and what will it cost?

3. What benefits will the company derive in terms of
   a. Customer service?
   b. Service to the systems users in the organization?
   c. Management information and decision making?

4. Will these better services offset the cost of installing a computer?

Very simply, can increased profit combined with cost savings offset the cost of developing the new systems?

MINI-CASE 1.3

Mr. O'Connor, the president of Double Duty Copying Company, was impressed with your summary on decision making for a computer installation. He has sent you the following memo:

TO:
FROM: F. J. O'Connor
DATE: Jan. 14, 19--
RE: Computer Possibilities
   Your summary regarding the pros and cons of installing a computer was most informative. Please forward to me by next Friday a brief summary (no more than one page) of the steps we must take to install a computer system.

• GROUP PROBLEM 1.1 •

Super-Quality Markets is a comparatively new firm in the retailing grocery business. Super-Quality was founded 6 years ago with two stores in the Los Angeles area. The company is expanding to 10 stores throughout southern California.

You have been with Super-Quality Markets for 5 years, originally as an accountant and now as controller, and you have watched the company grow from 30 employees to nearly 450. John Troast, Super-Quality's president, has had many conversations with you concerning the advisability of the corporation acquiring its own data processing equipment. Until now, much of the company's data processing work has been done either manually or through renting time on another company's computer.

Last week, Mr. Troast formally approved your recommendation to rent a small computer within the next 18 months. You have been appointed chairman of the committee to select and prepare for the computer.

Systems techniques are virtually unknown at Super-Quality Markets. The accounting systems, which you created, are all manual. They have been adequate, but you realize that soon the clerical staff will be unable to handle the volume. Without automation, the company will be greatly limited in its expansion program.

You and the members of your group are to act as the selection committee for Super-Quality Markets. The following agenda has been published for your first meeting.

1. Organize the committee.
2. Formulate the criteria for future committee decisions.
3. Discuss systems proposals.

One person from your group will be appointed by the instructor as committee chairman and he will conduct the first meeting of the committee. What other organizing does the committee require?

When the group has been organized, it should specify in writing how it will determine priorities. Mr. Troast expects a written statement concerning priorities following the meeting.

The committee has received two memos to consider at its first meeting. Review them before participating in the discussion.

Conduct the meeting. Document the results of your discussion, stating clearly the committee's action on each suggestion.

FROM THE DESK OF: Ed Dehler

Our recent conversation about priorities for the forthcoming computer system leads me to some serious thinking about our current and future needs. I feel very strongly that Super-Quality Markets badly needs an accurate inventory, updated daily. Our store managers universally feel that they could increase gross sales by 5 percent if only they knew the status of merchandise in the warehouses on a daily basis. Our current system, which provides monthly inventory status, is virtually useless to the store managers.

I suggest that inventory control be given the highest priority in the developing computer system.

FROM THE DESK OF: Martha Ryshus

Last week, four of our store clerks did not receive their paychecks. Moreover, the overtime payroll was not ready on time and many employees went through the weekend without money they had earned and were expecting. As I am sure you remember, we received a warning from the state government last February for late filing of the W-2 forms. Quite frankly, our employees cannot understand why it takes 7 working days to produce payroll checks after the pay period is completed.

The anticipated arrival of a computer at Super-Quality presents us with an opportunity to improve many areas. I realize full well that our foremost goals must be to reduce cost and provide profit, but an important way of achieving these objectives is by satisfying the needs of our employees. Morale in the organization is good, but a more timely and error-free payroll will go a long way toward improving the overall efficiency of the work force. I hope that payroll will be ranked highly in your considerations for conversion to a computerized system.

glossary

control   process of establishing procedural steps and check points to assure the accuracy and timeliness of data

conversion   process of changing from an existing data processing system to a new one

data base   all the data processing files relating to a specific aspect of the business

debugging   process of clearing up the minor problems in a system

feasibility study   systems project for determining the best plan for solving a company's problem

file   collection of related records

MIS   management information system; usually computer-based and designed to provide management with the information it requires to make profitable decisions

module   portion, or component, of a system

parameter   logical limit to the quantity of an item of data

PERT   Project Evaluation and Review Technique; management tool for scheduling complex problems

procedure   series of steps for carrying out repetitive operations

programmer   data processing professional who writes the instructions through which a computer executes data processing functions

programmer-analyst   data processing professional who performs the functions of solving corporate problems and programming these solutions for the computer

system   series of related procedures designed to achieve a business goal

systems analyst   data processing professional who examines business problems and formulates solutions to them

systems specification   document defining the principal aspects of a data processing system

systems study   project to design in detail a solution to a corporate problem

total system   system where all the resources of an organization are coordinated to achieve management's goals

user   anyone who receives output from the system or provides input for it

REVIEW QUESTIONS

1. List the steps in the systems development cycle.

2. What is meant by the term "life cycle of a system"?

3. Discuss two limitations in undertaking systems studies.

4. What factors must be considered by the selection committee in evaluating requests for systems changes?

5. What are some of the characteristics of a business system?

6. What levels of systems sophistication exist today?

7. What information would a systems specification usually contain?

8. What is the role of management in systems development?

9. What skills should a systems department possess?

10. List some typical systems users.

11. List five business situations in which you think a systems request can arise.

12. Describe the evolution of today's business systems from the time of World War II.

13. What is a management information system? How does it differ from other systems?

14. Comment on the following statement: "Systems analysts are creative geniuses and technical experts."

15. What is a total system? Give an example of one.

16. List five components of a system.

17. Comment on the following statement: "A system is a collection of computer programs."

18. What is a feasibility study?

19. What is meant by the phrase "limited human resources" in initiating systems studies?

20. What is the difference between a computer programmer and a systems analyst?

21. Ultimately, who decides whether a system is operating adequately or not?

part II

Systems
Techniques

chapter **2**

Hardware and Systems

Objectives

In Chapter 1, you learned that a system is a group of procedures used to accomplish a goal. In today's business environment, virtually all systems require
equipment, usually a computer, to function.

Since most business data are contained on one of three types of storage
media—punched cards, magnetic tape, and direct access devices—various pieces
of equipment, or hardware, are used to process this information. Each has its
own characteristics, its own advantages and disadvantages.

You will learn in this chapter that although data on magnetic tape are
read and written much faster, and are more economical to store, they are
processed basically the same way as data on punched cards. Both tape and cards
must be processed sequentially, that is, one record at a time in numerical (or
alphabetical) order. Direct access devices, such as the magnetic disk, may receive data or retrieve it in either sequential or random order.

The traditional bottleneck in processing data is in transferring information into machine-readable form. This chapter will explain the use of many of
the devices that can punch or scan information so that it can be read by a
machine.

Hardware is the term for the equipment comprising a data processing installation. It includes all EAM (electromagnetic accounting machines) equipment and all input/output and memory devices of the computer. Hardware largely determines the degree of systems sophistication possible at an installation.

THE EAM SYSTEM: UNIT RECORD EQUIPMENT

EAM, or unit record equipment, usually has one record on each card, so the terms EAM and unit record have become synonymous. An EAM system, in its simplest form, has one machine sort punched cards in numerical order, a second check the order of the cards, and a third print a report. These are the basic pieces of EAM equipment and their functions:

   sorter—arranges cards in numerical or alphabetical order, selects cards by using codes

   collator—merges or matches two files of cards, checks the sequence of cards, selects cards by codes

   interpreter—prints information on a card

   reproducer—copies all or some of the punches in one card onto another

   calculator—performs the arithmetic functions of an EAM system

   tabulator—adds, subtracts, and prints reports

   keypunch—punches data into a card

   verifier—checks the data the keypunch has put into a card

To develop an effective system with unit record equipment, the systems analyst must coordinate the clerical staff, which prepares the source documents and uses the systems reports with the machine operators, who handle the cards and carry out the systems procedures.

Unit record equipment has several limitations:

   one input and storage medium—EAM systems are restricted to the use of punched cards.

   numerous steps—Even the simplest jobs require several steps. This necessitates extensive card handling by machine operators, a frequent source of errors in a system.

   lack of speed—Unit record equipment is slow.

   simple operations only—When compared with computers, the potential of unit record equipment to do complex operations is very limited.

The advantage of unit record equipment is that it is far cheaper than computers to buy or rent. It is appropriate in small installations and in those which are just beginning to use automated equipment.

Figure 2-1 is a simple customer billing system designed for an oil-home-delivery company. Trace these steps through the chart to see whether or not you understand the system.

1. Delivery tickets for each oil delivery are keypunched and key-verified.

2. A preliminary register is printed to edit the punched data.

3. The keypunched input transaction cards are sorted by the grade of oil delivered and the customer number.

4. The transaction cards are merged with a "customer price file," which contains the rates each customer pays for the various grades of oil.

    a. Unmatched masters represent customers who had no transactions in this batch.

    b. Merged cards for customers who had transactions.

    c. Unmatched detail cards are either mistakes or new customers who do not have a master price card.

5. The price data from the customer price master are punched into the transaction cards.

6. A sorter separates the price masters from the transactions.

7. The customer price master file is put back together on a collator.

8. The amount to be billed is calculated on each transaction card.

9. The header cards for each customer, containing customer name, customer address, and miscellaneous data, are merged with the transaction cards.

10. Bills are printed on a tabulator.

11. The transaction cards are separated from the header cards on a sorter.

12. The header file is reconstructed.

COMPUTER SYSTEMS

Each major computer manufacturer has a full range of sizes and models of computer systems. For example, the IBM Corporation offers computer systems ranging from the small System/3 to some very large models of System 370.

System/3 is designed for the small business with a limited amount in its annual budget for computer rental. A typical System/3 configuration consists of a card reader-punch, a central processing unit (with as little as 8,000 positions of core), and a printer. Its advantage over a unit record system is that it is a computer and has a central memory with the flexibility of handling a variety of programs. System/3 is rapidly making traditional unit record equipment obsolete.

IBM also offers its System 360 Model 20 for the small user. Originally, the 360/20 was a card-oriented system, but now it may be used with magnetic tapes and direct access devices. The IBM 360 line includes Models 30 and 40 for the medium-sized user, and Models 50 and 65 for the larger user. Other models of the 360 series are available for specialized uses.

The IBM 370 series is newer and faster than its 360 counterparts. It also facilitates the use of larger and more efficient direct access devices and more sophisticated operating systems.

Other manufacturers, such as Honeywell, NCR, UNIVAC, and Control Data, produce comparable hardware.

The systems analyst encounters hardware systems on two levels. First, he often participates in studies to determine which manufacturer and model would be appropriate for his company. Second, when a specific model has been installed, the systems analyst must decide how the hardware system can best be utilized to meet the needs of his organization. Thus he must be very familiar with the potential and limitations of the system at his own installation.

BASIC STORAGE MEDIA

Two types of storage are used with computers: internal, which is the memory in the central processing unit, and external, which are the various media designed to contain data. The three main types of external storage are punched cards, magnetic tape, and direct access. Each type of external storage has special hardware for handling input and output.

Punched Card Systems

Card-oriented computer systems have these characteristics:

sequential processing—Card files must be processed sequentially. Thus before cards enter the system, they must be sorted into numerical (or alphabetic) order.

human involvement—Card systems require more human intervention than do other systems and thus are more prone to error.

record misplacement—A card record may be misplaced or missorted. This cannot be physically done with tape, disk, or drum.

time-consuming updating—Card files are kept current through updating (Fig. 2-2). To update a master file of 100,000 cards, the operator must process

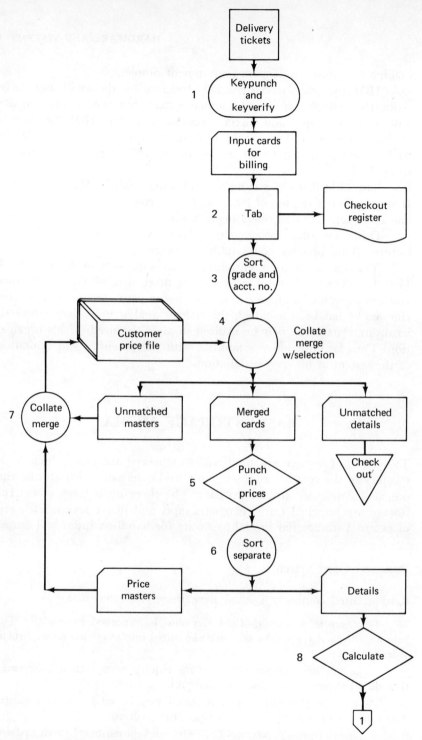

Fig. 2-1 Unit record billing system.

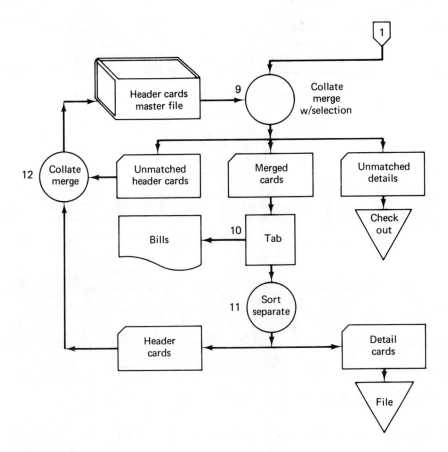

Fig. 2-1 Continued.

the original 100,000-card master file plus the input transactions. The card punch would produce an additional 100,000 output cards. Since a typical card punch unit punches approximately 300 cards per minute, it would take over 5 hours to update a file of this size, even if everything went smoothly.

    economy—Hardware for card-oriented files is more economical to rent or purchase; thus card systems are very common in small installations.

    lack of speed—The card reader is slower than other input devices, and its companion device, the card punch, is even slower.

Magnetic Tape Systems

Because punched card systems are slow and clumsy, the data processing industry developed magnetic tape as a storage device in the early 1950s.

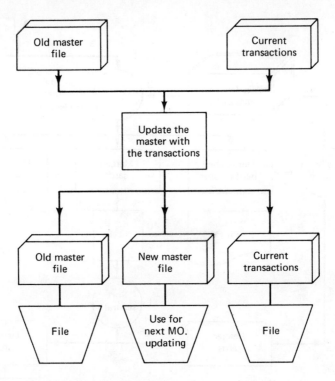

Fig. 2-2 Updating punched card files.

Magnetic tape has two basic advantages over punched cards:

1. Greater efficiency as a storage medium; a standard reel of tape about 1 foot in diameter can contain as much information as nearly half a million punched cards. Thus tape is far more efficient than cards for storing data.

2. Faster as an input/output device; tape is much faster than cards for processing information. For instance, a standard inch of tape contains 1,600 characters, or the data contained in 20 punched cards. Some tape drives read up to 200 inches of tape per second.

As in punched card systems, files in a tape system must be processed sequentially. Both a tape master file and the transactions being processed against it must be in the same order. This limitation becomes significant when information must be added to or extracted from a file. For example, if sales information on customer number 763 is needed, records number 1 through 762 must be read before the data are extracted. Even then, the tape must be rewound before other work may be processed.

The apparent advantage of magnetic tape as a storage medium is limited because a record must be physically separated from other records by a gap. When a tape record is read or written upon, the tape drive requires about ¾ inch of tape to start and stop. In determining the capacity of a tape file, the following factors must be considered:

record length: number of characters in each record
tape density: number of characters that will fit on 1 inch of tape
reel length: number of feet in a reel of tape
gap length: amount of tape required to start and stop a tape drive

How many records will fit on a length of magnetic tape with these specifications?

record length: 400 characters
tape density: 1,600 characters per inch
reel length: 2,400 feet
gap length: ¾ inch

A portion of the tape would look as shown in Figure 2-3.

Remember that each record contains 400 characters and that each inch of tape has a capacity of 1,600 characters. Thus each inch of tape contains one record of ¼ inch and an interrecord gap of ¾ inch. If each inch contains 1 record, then

```
      1 inch          =              1 record
    × 12 inches                    × 12
    ──────────                     ──────────
      1 foot          =              12 records
  × 2,400  feet/reel              × 2,400
  ──────────                      ──────────
    2,400  feet       =            28,800  records
```

Obviously, a tape file in which most of the tape contains gaps in-

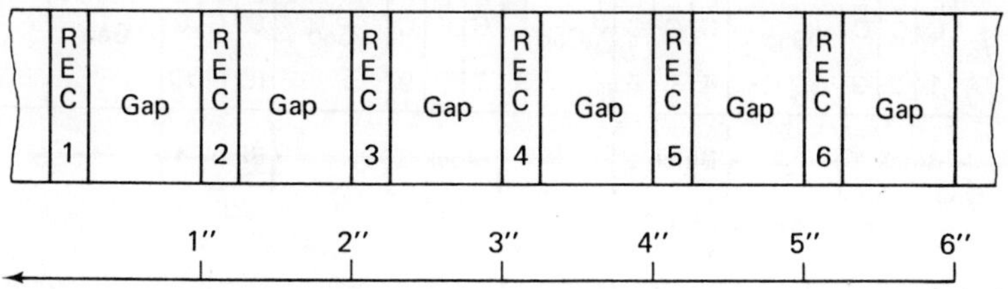

Figure 2-3

stead of data is highly inefficient. Therefore, records are grouped into blocks and several records are placed between gaps.

Consider this problem:

record length:	400 characters
tape density:	1,600 characters per inch
reel length:	2,400 feet
gap length:	¾ inch
blocking factor:	3 (3 records are contained between each gap)

A portion of the tape would look as shown in Fig. 2-4, which illustrates that 3 inches of tape now contains six records and two gaps. Now at least the tape contains half data and half gaps. Thus

$$
\begin{array}{rclcrcl}
3 \text{ inches} & & & = & & & 6 \text{ records} \\
\times\ 4 & & & & & & \times\ 4 \\
\hline
1 \text{ foot} & & & = & & & 24 \text{ records} \\
\times\ 2{,}400 & & & & & & \times\ 2{,}400 \\
\hline
2{,}400 \text{ feet} & & & = & & & 57{,}600 \text{ records}
\end{array}
$$

By changing the blocking factor from 1 to 3, the capacity of the tape was doubled.

The limitation on block length is the availability of the internal storage capacity of the central processing unit and the size of the programs the file will be used with. If a computer has 16,000 positions of storage and uses 12,000 in the instruction portion of a program, 4,000 positions remain for input/output handling. If the program calls for reading and writing tape files, the maximum block length for input or output would be 2,000 characters.

A tape system operates in the same general way as a card system. An

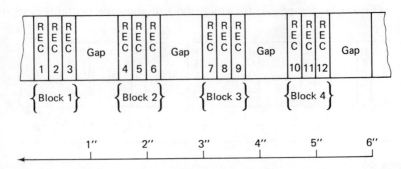

Figure 2-4

existing master file and the transactions being applied to it must be processed in numerical order. In a tape-oriented system, the master files are contained on magnetic tape; the transactions may be on either magnetic tape or punched cards. The computer program applies each transaction to the corresponding record in the master file, producing an updated master record. Tape systems have the advantage of reducing human intervention in a system, thus reducing errors.

Direct Access Systems

The magnetic disk, and its related devices, the drum and the data cell, provide tremendous potential for processing data, thus creating an additional challenge for the systems analyst. Hardware devices employing the disk concept are capable of directly accessing any record within a file. When information for customer number 763 is required, the computer can go directly to that record and extract it in less than 1 second, instead of the minutes, or perhaps hours, required with tape.

The three basic types of direct access storage devices (Fig. 2-5) are the magnetic drum, the disk, and the magnetic film strip. The magnetic drum looks like a rotating barrel with tracks around its circumference for data recording. Specific tracks on the drum are accessed by a row of read/write heads for recording or retrieving data as the tracks rotate past the heads.

The magnetic disk (Fig. 2-6) is similar to a group of phonograph records stacked vertically about 1 inch apart. The disk has a cluster of access arms capable of reading any "groove" or track on any surface. Some disks are permanently fixed within a housing called a disk drive; others may be removed to increase flexibility.

Magnetic film strips, such as IBM's data cell and NCR's CRAM, use a large number of film strips containing data in magnetized spots. The film strips are held in containers on a rotating carousel (Fig. 2-7). When the desired strip passes the read/write station, it is wrapped around a drum and may be read or written upon.

Direct access systems have several problems. They are generally more expensive than tape systems and more difficult to organize. Systems work, programming, and coordinating the human resources within an organization are extremely complex in a direct access system.

A direct access system represents a major departure from the processing concepts of both card and tape systems. It still provides the ability to operate in the same fashion as cards and tape: you can still group, sort, and process the transactions sequentially by batch processing. However,

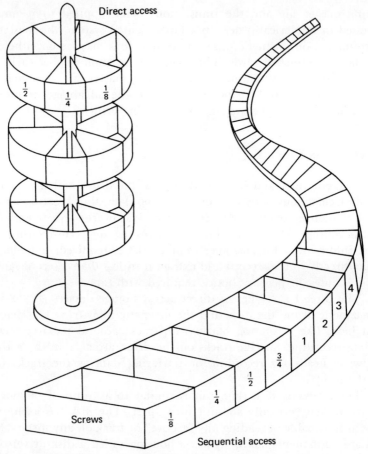

Fig. 2-5 Direct versus sequential access.

with a disk any record may be read or changed directly, as long as the disk is connected to the computer, by on-line processing.

UPDATING FILES

The concept of updating illustrates the contrast between direct access devices on one hand and magnetic tape and card files on the other. Files are dynamic and must be brought up to date regularly to reflect changes in status of items in the file.

Punched card and magnetic tape files are changed in essentially the

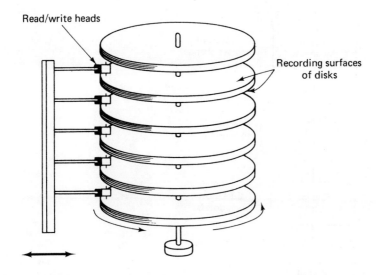

Read/write heads

Recording surfaces
of disks

Fig. 2-6 The disk concept.

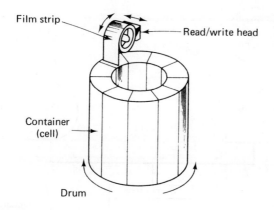

Film strip

Read/write head

Container
(cell)

Drum

Fig. 2-7 Carousel of the data cell.

same manner. Transactions are grouped into conveniently sized batches (Fig. 2-8) because processing them individually would be highly inefficient, and each batch of input transactions is then sorted into the same sequence as the master file. Next a record from the master file and the transaction file are read into the computer simultaneously and the computer is programmed to produce an updated master record for each current master record which has a corresponding transaction (Fig. 2-9).

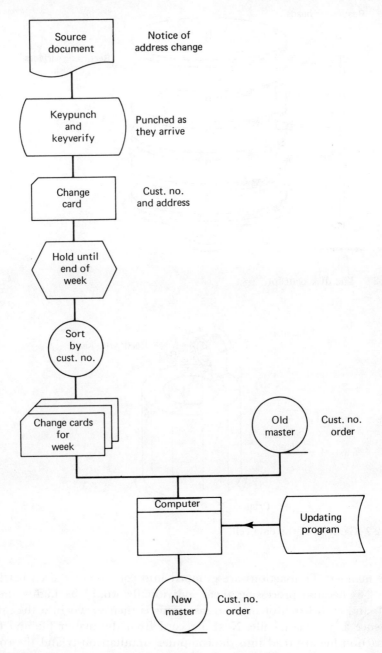

Fig. 2-8 Batch processing, using batches of one week's transactions.

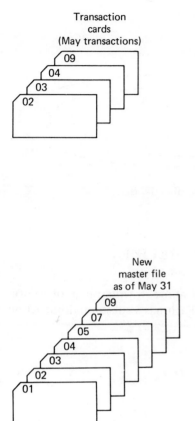

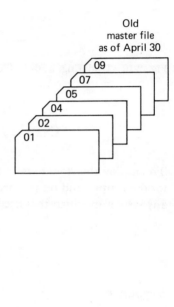

Fig. 2-9 Updating a card (or tape) file. Records 01, 05, and 07 are unchanged. Record 03 is a new record. Records 02, 03, 04, and 09 are changed in the new master file.

Existing master records with no corresponding transactions are directly copied onto the output master file. New master records may be added to the file by being introduced as transactions. When the process has been completed for all records. an entirely new output file has been created.

Direct access files may be changed more simply. Transactions need not necessarily be batched since the entire master file does not have to be read to change a record (Fig. 2-10). Input transactions are read and immediately applied to the master file regardless of where the current master record is located in the file. The characteristics of the various storage media are listed in Fig. 2-11.

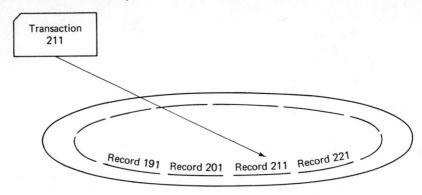

Fig. 2-10 Updating a disk file, transaction directly changes a master record.

INPUT/OUTPUT DEVICES

To employ the storage media mentioned above, a wide range of devices for data input and output are available. Each has a substantial impact on any system in which it is used.

PUNCH DEVICES

Keypunch

The keypunch is still the standard device for creating computer input. Its advantage is that almost every installation has had experience with it. Computer installations have a tendency to stay with basic hardware as long as possible since the introduction of newer devices causes immediate problems in retraining personnel.

The keypunch can put data only on a punched card, which we know is a slow and clumsy input medium. In a system using punched card input, one must punch the cards, check the accuracy of the data punched with a keyverifier, and sort the cards into numerical order before they enter the computer system. Each step risks human error.

Key-to-Tape Devices

Key-to-tape devices that put data directly onto magnetic tape are often used today to speed up processing input data. They enable the computer

	Cost	Speed	Updating
Cards	Comparatively chear	Slow, clumsy in handling	An entirely new file is produced
Tape	Moderate	Fast, but must be processed sequentially	An entirely new file is produced
Disk, drum, data cell	Expensive, particularly because difficult to organize	Very fast. Can get a particular item of data very quickly	The original file may be changed directly

Fig. 2-11 Characteristics of basic storage media.

system to read directly from the tape and take advantage of the increase in reading speed that a tape drive provides. The verification process is similar to keypunching in that an operator duplicates the original keying step, checking each element of data for accuracy. Unlike keypunching, this is done with the same machine on which the original data were produced. An advantage here is that as an error is detected, the correct data may be put directly on the tape, while a punched card containing an error must be destroyed and its entire content made over.

If the master file for a system using key-to-tape is on magnetic tape, the input tape must be sorted into the same order of the master file.

Today, it is possible to put keyed input directly onto a disk, permitting direct access and high-speed sorting of the input data. This allows a group of key-to-disk operators to put input data for several applications onto a disk simultaneously. The complexities and cost of organizing input on disks usually permits only large installations, with large volumes of input data to take advantage of this device.

Punched Paper Tape

Punched paper tape is another input medium. A paper tape punch can be attached to an electric typewriter, a cash register, or an adding machine to record data as a by-product of another operation. For example, a clerk may run an add tape of a batch of checks before depositing them in a bank. If the adding machine is connected to a paper tape punch, a tape containing each check amount and the total dollars to be deposited is produced simultaneously with the add tape. This paper tape can be read by a paper tape reader and its data entered into a computer system.

Punched paper tape has these advantages:

1. It can be produced as a by-product of another operation.

2. The length of each record on a tape is unlimited. The limit on a punched card is 80 characters.

3. Data on paper tape can be transmitted by telephone or telegraph lines. Two computers, located thousands of miles apart, can transmit data to each other if each has a paper tape reader and punch and if they are connected by telephone or telegraph wires. This has been the most successful application of punched paper tape.

Paper tape, however, has these disadvantages:

1. As an input/output medium, it is slower than punched cards.

2. Using paper tape as input requires additional hardware, the paper tape reader, and the paper tape punch, which are useful for only a few applications at an installation.

SCANNING DEVICES

Because creating computer input is costly, time consuming, and the cause of most of the errors in a system, much research has been done on the problem resulting in the development of scanning devices for reading data from its source directly into a computer.

A magnetic ink character reader (MICR) interprets specially formed characters on checks and has been used by the banking industry for years, primarily to sort checks rapidly. MICR readers generally are limited to numeric characters, as indicated in Fig. 2-12, and the location of these

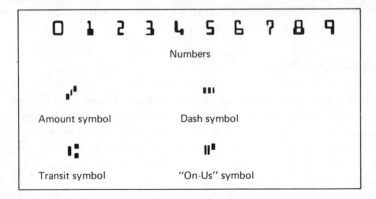

Fig. 2-12 Magnetic ink characters.

numbers on the source document is predetermined. Most readers require that magnetic ink characters be at the bottom $\frac{1}{4}$ inch of the source document.

A variety of optical character readers (OCR) are available for bypassing the keypunch step. An OCR device reads a limited number of both numerical and alphabetical characters. The standard type font (United States of America Standards Institute) is shown in Fig. 2-13. OCR devices capable of reading human printing are available, but individuality in handwriting causes problems and limits the application of such devices.

The obvious advantage of OCR equipment is that it bypasses keypunching and thus saves time and money. To offset these savings, there is the problem of cost; the monthly rental of optical scanners ranges from $2,000 to $20,000. They also have other drawbacks:

1. Design limitation of documents; style of printing and location of characters on a page are quite restricted.

2. Verification; if the source document is completed incorrectly, it is difficult to check the errors.

OUTPUT DEVICES

The standard computer output device remains the high-speed printer. But as computers became more sophisticated, it was necessary to present data more meaningfully and thus the data processing industry developed various graphic display devices.

The cathode ray tube (CRT) is a television tube that can display any data a printer can print. Moreover, the cathode ray tube displays data as either printed characters, lines, or pictures.

A light pen may be used to alter pictorial data. The light pen provides the computer with input to change the data it contains. For instance, in engineering, a light pen can change the design of a bridge projected on a cathode ray tube, as the light's impulses will be the input for constructing a new design.

The typewriter terminal has become a standard input/output device for computers. Many terminals may be connected with a computer to update a master file as transactions occur. A tyewriter terminal is a tyewriter connected to a computer by telephone lines. Thus it can transmit and receive data.

The advantages of a typewriter terminal are that it can capture data immediately as transactions occur. The key strokes that were used to type sources documents for use by keypunch operations can now be

Alphabet (upper case)

ABCDEFGHIJKLMNOPQRSTUVWXYZ

Alphabet (lower case)

abcdefghijklmnopqrstuvwxyz

Numerics

0123456789

Symbols

•	Period	—	Minus or hyphen	ʬ	Quotation mark
˥	Comma	⁏	Colon	✳	Asterisk
?	Question mark	+	Plus sign	=	Equals sign
/	Slant or slash	⅟	Percent sign	˥	Semi colon
{	Left parenthesis	$	Dollar sign	'	Apostrophe
}	Right parenthesis	&	Ampersand		

Fig. 2-13 Standard OCR symbols.

transported directly to the computer. Moreover, decision makers in an organization need no longer wait for the computer to print out reports on the activity of the organization. When the data are organized properly on a direct access device, and the inquiry programs have been written, a corporate decision maker may extract from the company's file the precise information he requires by typing an inquiry and receiving a response on his typewriter terminal. Typewriter terminals are only effective when they are on-line with files on direct access devices.

Other graphic display devices include the graph plotter and audio response units.

MINI-CASE 2.1

The Brewer Brothers Brewery, Inc., brews and distributes beer throughout the north-central states. Brewer Brothers produces two types of beer: Style, a high-priced premium, and the economically priced Brewers Beer. The beer is sold to bars and other retail outlets for domestic consumption. Both brands are sold in cans, bottles, and draft through the Brewer Brothers sales force of 50 salesmen.

Sales analysis figures are currently compiled quarterly. Each salesman's daily sales sheets are totaled on an adding machine each quarter, and a report is typed showing each salesman's sales per month, his total quarterly sales, and the total sales for the company. All sales are totaled by product.

Last year, Brewer Brothers ventured into computerized data processing for the first time by installing a third-generation computer. The configuration consists of a central processing unit with 64,000 positions of storage, four tape drives, two disk packs, a printer, a card reader, and a card punch. The company's payroll has been computerized successfully and now management has decided to look into producing some meaningful sales analysis figures. The basic data for the system will come from an accounts receivable system that is currently being installed. Management expects the new system to produce sales quotas, sales commissions, and sales trend analyses for management.

The company has asked you to do some preliminary work in determining whether or not the hardware installed is appropriate for the job.

List five questions that you wish to ask management.

Describe the type of sales information you feel would be required by management.

What hardware would be required to produce the type of data you suggest?

What would you recommend as the basic storage medium?

Is the current hardware configuration sufficient?

MINI-CASE 2.2

The master record for the 8,000 checking accounts of Frugal National Bank will contain 400 characters. A program is being written that will list information from this file on a monthly basis. The program will have a maximum of 3,600 positions for reading input data.

The file will be recorded on 2,400-foot reels. The tape drive requires ¾-inch interblock gaps. The tape density is 1,600 characters.

On the basis of this information only, determine

1. The appropriate blocking factor.
2. How many reels of tape will be required to contain the file?

• GROUP PROBLEM 2.1 •

The Paramount Oil Company delivers oil to over 18,000 customers in a large city and its suburbs in the northeastern United States. Most of the customers are private homeowners; others are stores and small businesses.

Paramount Oil is a family-owned business that has grown quite large over the past 10 years. It now owns 50 trucks and employs over 350 people.

Billing has always been a problem at Paramount. During the winter, bills are often sent to the customer three or four weeks late. Four years ago, Paramount installed two bookkeeping machines for customer billing, but they have been unable to keep up with the increased volume of business.

The current billing system uses a manually prepared delivery ticket as the basic source document. When the driver makes an oil drop, he fills in the customer's name, customer number, the amount of the drop, and the price per gallon. Ordinarily, each customer receives several drops per month during the cold season. The delivery tickets are individually posted to the customer's ledger card by the bookkeeping machine. Customer remittances are also machine-posted to the same ledger card. At month end, the bookkeeping machine determines the customer's balance, and a carbon copy of the ledger card is sent to the customer as a bill.

Clerical accuracy is a serious problem. Last month, 3 percent of the customers billed complained that they were overcharged. There were no complaints of undercharging.

The prospects for expanding the business are good. The sales manager estimates that there will be 24,000 customers by the end of next year because of new housing in the suburbs. It looks now as if the billing department will not be able to handle the increased volume effectively with the existing equipment. To add to the problem, the company has just announced that it is in the process of acquiring a chain of 10 gasoline stations.

Peter Paramount, the company president, has asked you to make some preliminary suggestions for a hardware configuration. He emphasized that he has no preconceived opinions and that he is only seeking suggestions for the company's management to study. However, in a recent memo he itemized what he expects the new system to accomplish. His list and some of his comments:

clerical accuracy—"We are losing money because our system cannot handle the volume. Our customers are losing confidence in us."

audit trail—"I want to know that when a driver writes that he put 50 gallons in Johnson's tank, that 50 gallons went in."

improved cash flow—"We must have better followup for those customers who pay late or do not pay at all."

corporate efficiency—"We now have 50 trucks zigzagging all over this area. I am sure that better equipment and better systems can improve scheduling."

improving other systems—"We can do all our accounting on the new equipment. Payroll . . . payables . . . possibly even inventory."

Suggest a hardware configuration for Paramount Oil. Remember that the company is only at the beginning of its planning and is looking for creative ideas rather than solutions. Specify in your recommendations a basic storage medium and the input/output devices that you feel will be required to satisfy the needs of Paramount Oil.

glossary

CPU central processing unit; main frame of the computer, which contains the internal storage and the circuitry for performing arithmetic and logical functions

CRT a cathode ray tube; a television tube used for displaying computer output

direct access a process in which any record in a file may be located without reading through all the preceding records in the file

EAM punched card data processing equipment which uses one card for each record in a file. The term is used in this book as a synonym for unit record

hardware various pieces of equipment that make up a computer configuration

key-to-tape punch device that encodes input data directly on magnetic tape

MICR magnetic ink character recognition—a system where input documents may be read by a device that can detect magnetic qualities in special inks

OCR optical character recognition—an input device that reads characters conforming to predetermined shapes

operating system series of programs, written by the computer manufacturer, which assists the computer in executing applications programs and in performing input/output functions

sequential processing system that processes master files and transactions in numerical order

software programs and programming routines used to extend the capacity of the computer

updating process of making files current by applying transactions to an existing master file

unit record synonym for EAM equipment—a system that uses one punched card for each record in a file

REVIEW QUESTIONS

1. What are the three basic types of storage media?

2. What are the advantages of key-to-tape input over punched card input? What are the disadvantages?

3. Explain the concept of updating.

4. What do you see as the developing trends in producing data input?

5. Do you feel that key-to-tape devices will make keypunching obsolete? Give three reasons for your answer.

6. How popular do you think the key-to-disk devices will become? What advantages do they have? What are their disadvantages?

7. What are some of the disadvantages of EAM equipment? What advantage does it have?

8. List five characteristics of punched card systems.

9. What advantages does magnetic tape have over punched cards as a storage medium?

10. What do you think is the impact of direct access devices upon the data processing industry?

11. Where can punched paper tape be used advantageously?

12. OCR devices have obvious advantages over keypunching. Why are they not used by all companies?

13. Comment on this statement: "Unit record equipment is obsolete today."

14. List five pieces of unit record equipment and describe their functions.

15. What type of knowledge must a systems analyst have concerning computer hardware?

16. Why are tape records blocked?

17. What is a blocking factor?

18. What are the main types of direct access storage devices?

19. List four ways in which computer output may be displayed today.

20. What is the impact of terminals and direct access storage devices on corporate decision making?

Basic Tools in
Systems Analysis: I

Objectives

In Chapters 3 and 4 you will learn to use the basic tools that systems analysts employ. Chapter 3 deals with display tools, tools that picture information graphically for easier analysis. Chapter 4 explains how decision-making tools are used.

The most fundamental systems tool is the flowchart. You will learn to display a system using the standard flowcharting symbols for both clerical and computer-oriented systems.

Some information is better displayed with a decision table, especially when there is a series of alternative actions to be taken depending upon the result of the test of certain conditions. Other data, such as a schedule of events, lend themselves more to display in a Gantt chart. You will learn to do both in this chapter.

THE BASIC TOOLS

The systems analyst has a variety of tools available to help him do his job. These tools fall into two general categories; display tools and decision-making tools.

The most fundamental tools of the systems analyst are devices to display data. A systems analyst must display the systems with which he is working so that he can effectively organize data to facilitate analysis and decision making and convey his ideas to the user, corporate management, and other systems professionals (Fig. 3-1).

Display tools include

1. Systems flowcharts
2. Programming flowcharts
3. Decision tables
4. Gantt charts

Also available are a series of techniques designed to assist the decision-making process of an organization. These include

1. PERT charts
2. Linear programming
3. Simulation

Other systems analysis tools exist, but most are variations of the ones mentioned. Moreover, PERT charts may be considered either a display or a decision-making tool, depending upon how sophisticated an organization is in their use.

The systems analyst uses tools to:

Organize data for — Analysis / Decision making

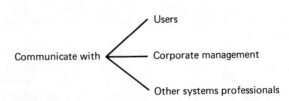

Communicate with — Users / Corporate management / Other systems professionals

Fig. 3-1 Use of systems tools.

SYSTEMS FLOWCHART

A flowchart has differing meanings and uses for various people in data processing. Here, we shall consider two types of flowcharts: the systems flowchart, which is essentially a diagram of the steps in a system, and a programming flowchart, or block diagram, which is a blueprint of the logical steps in a program.

Despite frequent efforts to standardize systems flowcharting, systems analysts seem to keep coming up with variations on the basic methods. Often a slight deviation from the basic symbols of a charting system is used to emphasize a particular point. So, in spite of efforts at standardization, innovation in charting will continue, and where it leads to better communications, it should be encouraged. However, it is only wise to innovate after the basic techniques have been mastered. Even then, modifying the standards risks a breakdown in communication.

We use two sets of charting symbols: one for charting noncomputerized clerical systems and one for charting computerized routines.

The symbols for clerical charting are illustrated in Fig. 3-2. For some idea of how the symbols are used, examine Figs. 3-3 and 3-4. See whether you understand this simple billing system.

This system of charting has several advantages. First, it has only a few symbols and is easier to teach the layman. It also forces the analyst to think out the ultimate disposition of every form in the system. It assists the analyst in highlighting the redundancies in a system and in exposing delay points. Finally, this type of chart often pinpoints inefficiencies in a system which are not apparent from a narrative description.

The following are some points to remember in flowcharting clerical operations:

    1. Lines should never cross. This confuses a reader.

    2. Put the document symbol on the chart wherever it is necessary to avoid confusion. This is especially true when two documents come together at

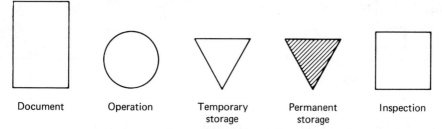

| Document | Operation | Temporary storage | Permanent storage | Inspection |

Fig. 3-2 Symbols for flowcharting clerical operations.

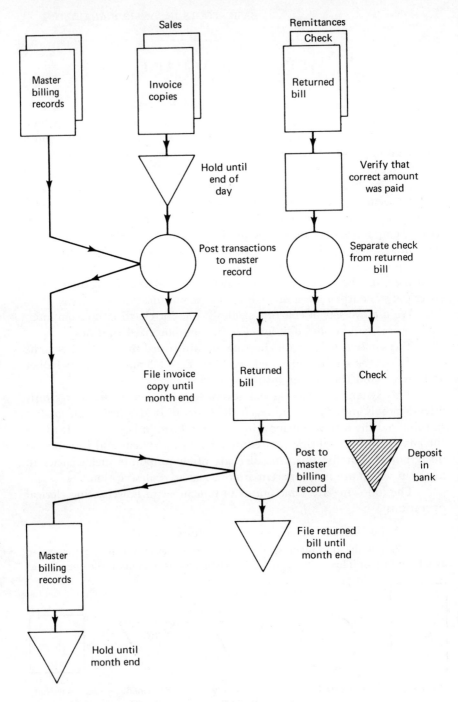

Fig. 3-3 Flowchart of the clerical operations in a daily billing system.

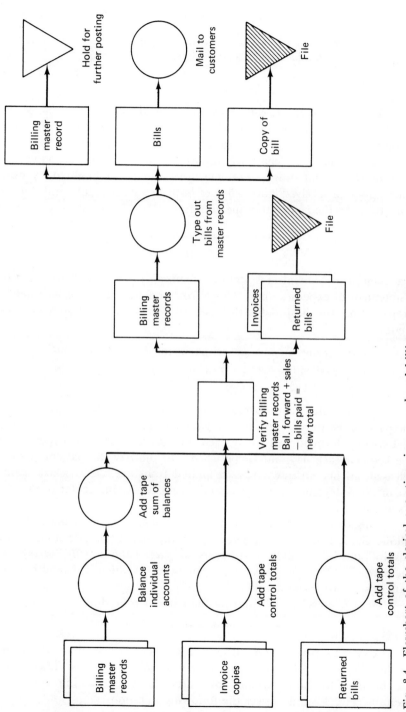

Fig. 3-4 Flowchart of the clerical operations in a month-end billing system.

53

one operating step.

3. Make notations simple, but clear. Remember, most charts serve both as systems documentation and as a user device.

4. Work flow can be displayed either horizontally or vertically, whichever is more appropriate for the data.

The basic flowchart can be expanded to illustrate other factors besides work flow. The problem of time can sometimes be a major factor in illustrating a systems problem and it can be introduced into a chart.

Annotations on a chart are important. Such vital factors as volume of transactions and unique problem areas can be highlighted by using annotations properly. Figure 3-5 uses both a time schedule and annotations to make the chart more meaningful.

MINI-CASE 3.1

The American General Hospital of Pittsburgh presents each patient with a statement of expenses upon release from the hospital. The statement is prepared on the hospital's IBM 360/30 computer. The statement includes:

1. The name, address, and telephone number of the patient
2. A detailed listing of every expense
3. A total of these expenses

The statement is prepared on the computer on the release date for the patient. However, the data are gathered daily, mostly from a Listing of Expenses form turned in by each floor supervisor. The expenses are checked out each day and keypunched. On the day the patient is to be released, all his expense cards are pulled from the file, checked against the original documents, and sent to the data processing center to produce a statement.

The identifying information on the statement comes from a Patient Admit Card, which is completed when the patient is admitted to the hospital and is eventually keypunched as part of the patient's record. All the cards in the system have a patient number which distinguishes one patient's records from another.

Draw a flowchart illustrating the current procedure.

A systems analyst normally uses a second set of symbols, illustrated in Fig. 3-6, when diagramming computer-oriented systems. This system can be used for both systems flowcharts and programming flowcharts. Examine Fig. 3-7 and answer the following questions:

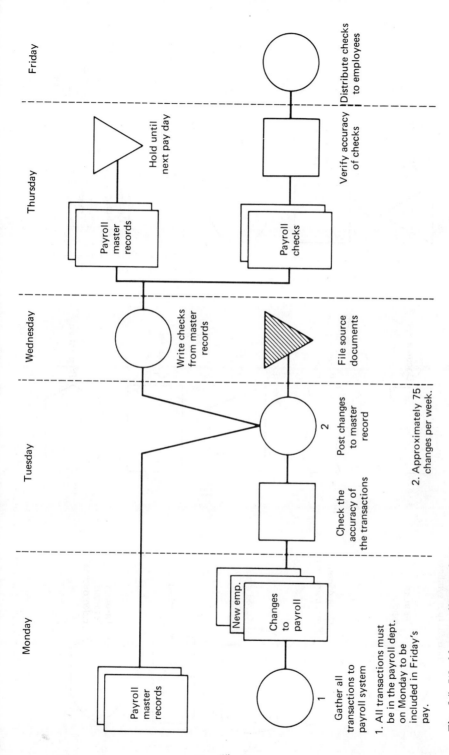

Fig. 3-5 Weekly payroll procedure.

55

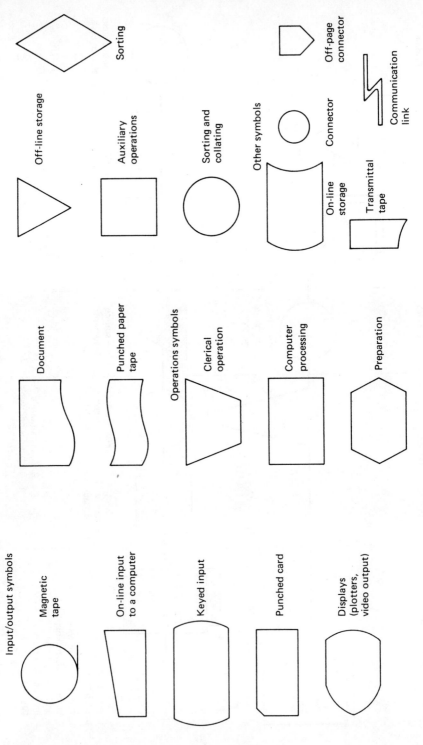

Fig. 3-6 Symbols for flowcharting a computer-based system.

Input/output symbols

Magnetic tape

On-line input to a computer

Keyed input

Punched card

Displays (plotters, video output)

Document

Punched paper tape

Operations symbols

Clerical operation

Computer processing

Preparation

Off-line storage

Auxiliary operations

Sorting and collating

Other symbols

On-line storage

Transmittal tape

Sorting

Off-page connector

Connector

Communication link

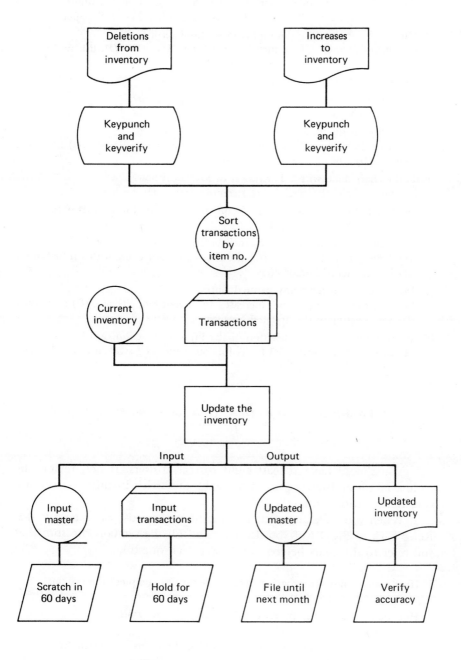

Fig. 3-7 Monthly inventory updating system.

1. The master file for this system is on which type of input medium?
   (A) magnetic tape *(B)* punched cards *(C)* disk packs *(D)* paper tape

2. On which medium are the input transactions recorded?
   (A) magnetic tape *(B)* punched cards *(C)* data cell *(D)* disk packs

3. How many programs are used in the system?
   (A) 1 *(B)* 2 *(C)* 3 *(D)* 4

4. Can this system be handled by unit record equipment?
   (A) yes *(B)* no

5. How large is the master file?
   (A) over 100,000 *(B)* the information is not in the chart *(C)* less than 50,000 *(D)* 1,000

6. Is the chart done with a horizontal or a vertical flow?
   (A) horizontal *(B)* vertical *(C)* combination *(D)* neither

7. What is the minimum number of tape drives required to do this system?
   (A) 1 *(B)* 2 *(C)* 3 *(D)* 4

8. How long is the master file retained before it is scratched?
   (A) 1 month *(B)* 60 days *(C)* the chart does not contain this information *(D)* it is scratched immediately

9. Does the system have any printed output in it?
   (A) yes, the deletions and increases to inventory *(B)* no *(C)* sometimes *(D)* yes, a listing of the updated inventory

10. What is the ultimate disposition of the input transaction cards?
    (A) filed permanently *(B)* held for 60 days *(C)* scratched in 30 days *(D)* thrown out immediately

ANSWERS: (1) *A*   (2) *B*   (3) *A*   (4) *B*   (5) *B*   (6) *B*   (7) *B*   (8) *B*   (9) *D*
(10) *B*

You should have at least eight correct answers. If not, review the basic symbols and try the problem again. Stay with it until you can answer ten questions correctly.

When you have answered ten questions correctly, examine Fig. 3-8. Refer back to Fig. 3-6 if you do not recall all the symbols. Be sure that you refer to the chart before you answer each question.

1. How many computer programs were necessary to complete the system?
   (A) 1 *(B)* 2 *(C)* 3 *(D)* 4

2. How many tape drives are required to carry out this system?
   (A) 1 *(B)* 2 *(C)* 3 *(D)* 4

3. On what piece of equipment is the step "Sort by batch no." performed?
   (A) computer *(B)* tape drive *(C)* interpreter *(D)* sorter

4. The list of those subscriptions that expire in 2 months is produced on a
   (A) printed listing *(B)* magnetic tape *(C)* disk pack *(D)* punched cards
5. What is the ultimate disposition of the subscription form?
   (A) it is keypunched, then never used *(B)* it is thrown away in 60 days
   (C) it is held for 1 month *(D)* it is filed
6. On which input/output medium is the master file contained?
   (A) punched cards *(B)* ledger cards *(C)* magnetic tape *(D)* disk packs
7. What function do the batch totals serve in the system?
   (A) none *(B)* to establish a control for the new subscriptions *(C)* to establish a control for the expiries *(D)* to establish a control total for both new
   subscriptions and expiries
8. After reviewing the chart, what are the first five questions you would ask to
   clarify the procedure illustrated?

ANSWERS: (1) *B*   (2) *D*   (3) *D*   (4) *B*   (5) *D*   (6) *C*   (7) *B*

Below are some suggestions that will be helpful in composing more meaningful flowcharts:

1. The flowchart for a system is only as good as the system analyst's ability to gather facts correctly. The chart has little value if it does not accurately portray what the current system is doing, or what a proposed system will do.

2. Using proper symbols is important because they give some universality to charting.

3. Arrows should be used whenever necessary to show the direction of the flow of work. However, when the direction of flow is obvious, the arrows may be omitted.

4. Notice in Fig. 3-8 the use of the "loop" to illustrate steps that can take place more than once in a procedure. In the example, if the control tape does not balance with the computer listing, the steps of finding and keypunching the errors are repeated until the two totals are checked out.

5. Note the use of page connectors in Fig. 3-8. The symbol ⛒ is used when the line being drawn continues on the next page. If the connection is on the same page, use a ◯.

6. Symbols are usually numbered consecutively in each flowchart.

7. Many systems analysts use different symbols, and this is sometimes confusing. Whenever a nonstandard symbol is used, it must be explained in a legend.

8. The purpose of flowcharting is to communicate ideas. To do this effectively, have someone review your chart to see whether he understands it. His questions will help you clarify the chart.

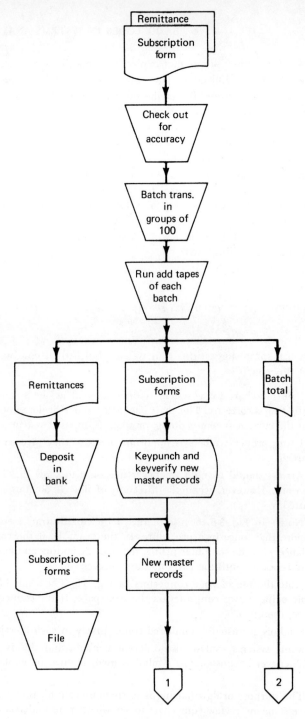

Fig. 3-8 Subscription system for the Leahy Magazine Publishing Co.

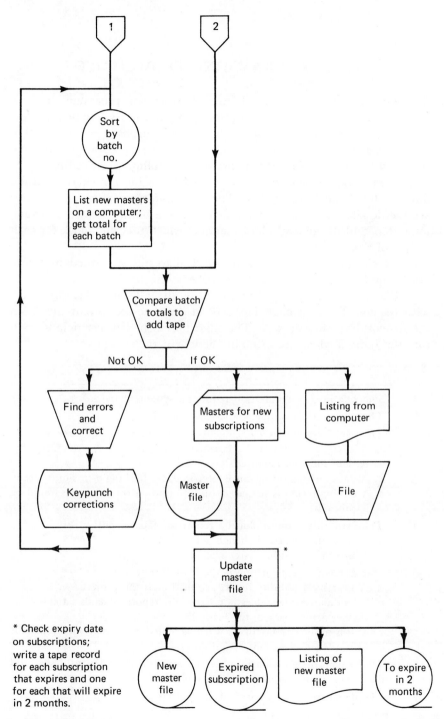

* Check expiry date
on subscriptions;
write a tape record
for each subscription
that expires and one
for each that will expire
in 2 months.

Fig. 3-8 Continued.

THE PROGRAMMING FLOWCHART

The symbols depicted in Fig. 3-6 may be used for programming flow-charts. A programming flowchart (block diagram) is a symbolic representation of the logic in a program. It has several purposes: communication of ideas between systems analysts and programmers, program documentation, and as an outline for the programmer to follow when coding.

Most programs lend themselves to a simpler form of charting, using only the five symbols in Fig. 3-9. The two basic types of block diagrams are the detailed block diagram, which uses one block for each programming step, and the general block diagram, which uses one block for each section of a program.

Developing the logic to write block diagrams is learned in a programming course and is beyond the scope of this book.

Flowcharts may be used to illustrate virtually any idea concerned with systems. Trace through Fig. 3-10 in detail to see how it illustrates the systems development cycle. The chart uses a shaded rectangle to indicate the individual or group taking action in the system.

Step	Action
1.	Someone in the organization requests a systems change.
2.	The selection committee studies the request.
3.	The selection committee documents its decision in one of three ways: a. A disapproval memo is returned to the requestor, explaining the reasons for the committee's action. b. An authorizing document is prepared, establishing a feasibility team. c. A tabling memo is prepared, outlining when future action would be appropriate.
4.	The feasibility team produces a report to management: a. It finds the suggested change not feasible, or b. It presents a feasible systems plan.
5.	Management accepts or rejects the feasibility report. a. A negative feasibility report accepted ends the project. b. When management does not accept the report, it sends a request for further action back to the feasibility team. c. A feasibility systems plan, when accepted by management, will be forwarded to a systems design group.
6.	The systems design team formulates a more detailed systems design and documents it in a systems specification.
7.	The design concept is accepted or rejected by user and corporate management.
8.	If rejected, the design concepts are reviewed and revised by the systems design group.

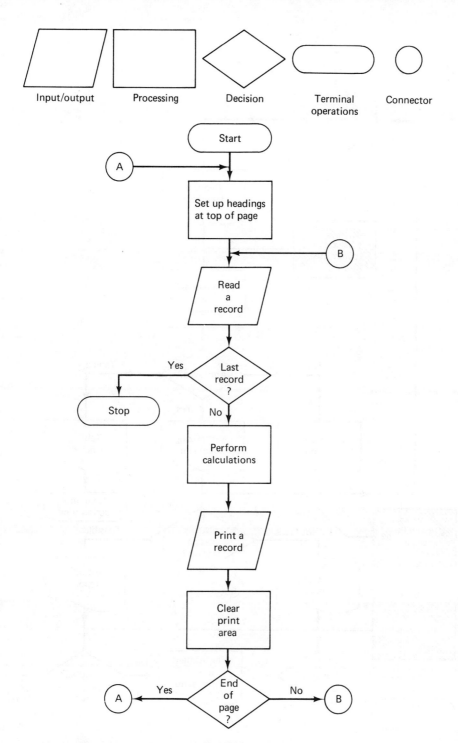

Input/output   Processing   Decision   Terminal operations   Connector

Start

A

Set up headings at top of page

B

Read a record

Last record ?   Yes

Stop   No

Perform calculations

Print a record

Clear print area

End of page ?   Yes → A   No → B

Fig. 3-9 General block diagram using only five symbols.

63

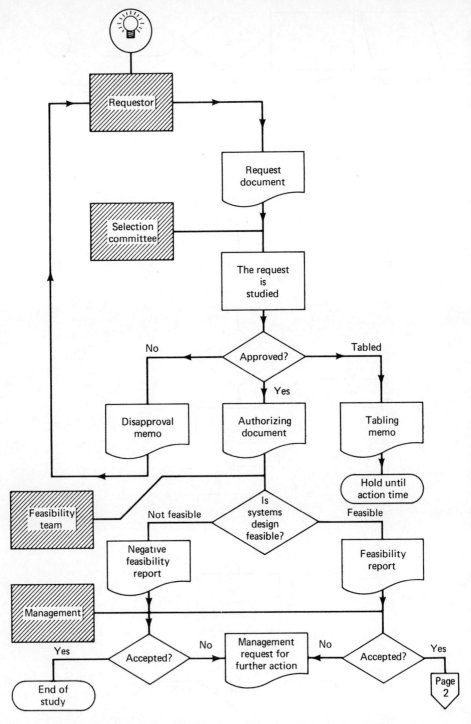

Fig. 3-10 Flowchart illustrating the systems development cycle.

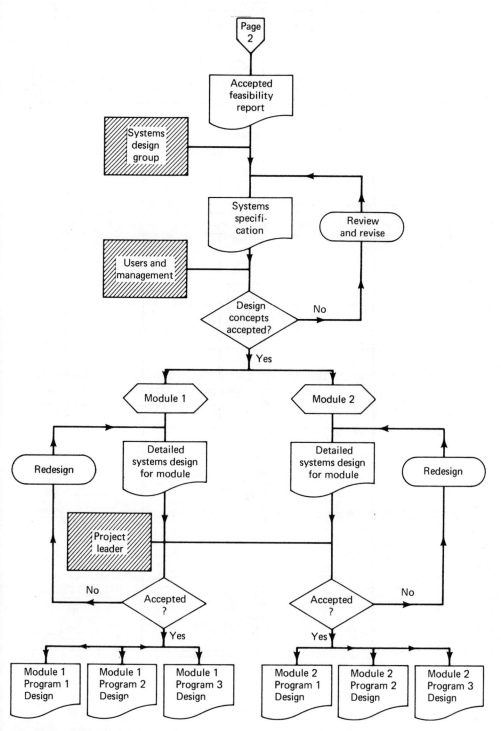

Fig. 3-10 Continued.

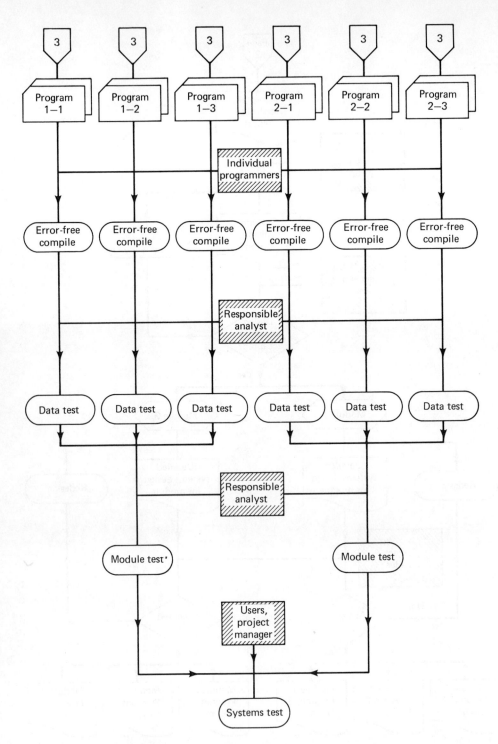

Fig. 3-10 Concluded.

9. If accepted, the project is divided into modules for detailed systems design.

10. The project leader decides whether the detailed systems design is acceptable.
    a. If it is not acceptable, the system is redesigned.
    b. When the detailed systems design is acceptable, the programs are designed.

11. The programs are written to compile without an error.

12. Each program is tested.

13. Each module is tested.

14. The system is tested.

DECISION TABLES

The decision table is a popular form for documenting programming problems. It is particularly appropriate when a program contains a series of conditions to be tested, the answer to the test determining the actions to be taken. The elementary form of the decision table, called a limited-entry table, is used for a program whose conditions may be answered by a simple "yes" or "no."

For example, a woman may be faced with three alternatives, depending upon her answers to these conditions:

1. If her fingernails are short and bitten, she will stop biting her nails.
2. If her nails are short and broken, she will use a nail conditioner.
3. If her nails are long and beautiful, she will leave the nails alone.

These three conditions, when answered by a yes or no, result in three different combinations. Expressed as a decision table, these alternatives look like this:

Conditions			
Nails are short and bitten	Yes	No	No
Nails are short and broken	No	Yes	No
Nails are long and beautiful	No	No	Yes
Actions			
Stop biting nails	*		
Get a nail conditioner		*	
Leave nails alone			*

To compose a decision table, a systems analyst must list in the upper left quadrant of the table, called the condition stub, all the conditions to be tested in the program. The lower left quadrant, the action stub, contains *all* possible actions that may be taken. In the upper right, the conditions entries quadrant, each condition is answered "yes" or "no." The appropriate action to be carried out for every combination of "yes" and "no" is then checked off in the lower right quadrant, the action entries quadrant.

Condition stub	Condition entries
Lists all the conditions to be tested	Answer each question "yes" or "no"
Action stub	Action entries
List all possible actions that may be taken	Check off the appropriate actions

MINI-CASE 3.2

A programmer must write a subroutine for a payroll program to calculate FICA tax. If the employee's year-to-date gross pay already exceeds $13,200, the program will skip the FICA calculation and proceed to subsequent routines.

When the year-to-date gross pay does not exceed $13,200, the current pay is added to the year-to-date gross pay and that sum is compared with $13,200. If the sum still does not exceed $13,200, the current pay is multiplied by the current FICA tax rate, giving the FICA tax for the current pay period. The program then proceeds to subsequent routines.

When the sum of the year-to-date gross pay plus the current salary exceeds $13,200, the year-to-date gross pay is subtracted from $13,200 and the remainder (taxable income) is multiplied by the current FICA rate. The program then proceeds to subsequent routines.

Express this problem in decision-table form.

Figure 3-11 is a solution to this problem.

The extended-entry table increases the potential of a decision table. In it, the condition entries are not merely yes or no replies but are extenuations of the questions. Contrast these two questions:

Is age greater than 30?

Is age <20, ≥ 20 and <30, ≥ 30 and <40, or ≥ 40 and <50?

Condition stub	Condition entries		
Ytd gross exceeds $13,200	Yes	No	No
Ytd gross + current salary is less than $13,200	—	Yes	No
Ytd gross + current salary is greater than $13,200	—	—	Yes
Action stub	Action entries		
Multiply current salary by current FICA rate		✓	
Subtract ytd gross from $13,200, giving taxable income			✓
Multiply taxable income by current FICA rate			✓
Proceed to subsequent routines	✓	✓	✓

Fig. 3-11 Decision table illustrating the FICA calculation subroutine.

The former is answered with a simple yes or no. The latter question is completed by the condition entries. When both types of questions are contained in the same decision table, it is referred to as a mixed-entry table.

MINI-CASE 3.3

The Student Council of Harper Valley Junior College wishes to make a statistical listing of all seniors. If the senior is a male, and a veteran, he will have a "V" printed after his name. A male student will have his marital status printed. If the student is female and single, she will have her name and phone number printed, if she is over 20 and less than 26 years old. Single females under 20 will only have their names printed. Single females, 26 and over, will have their date of birth printed. All married females will have their marital status printed.

Prepare a mixed-entry decision table to illustrate the logic in this problem. Compare your table with the one in Fig. 3-12.

Not every program can be expressed in a simple decision table. Most programs require several tables, each corresponding to a program subroutine. Programmers employ the DO and GO TO notations to exit one table and enter another. The DO notation will bring the logical flow to another table and return it to the point of departure from the original table. A GO TO notation will bring the flow of logic to another

Condition stub

Is student a senior?	Y	Y	Y	Y	Y	Y	Y	Y	N
Is student a male?	Y	Y	N	N	N	N	N	N	
Student's age?			< 20	> 19 and < 26	> 25	< 20	> 19 and < 26	> 25	
Is student a vet?	N	Y							
Is student single?			Y	Y	Y	N	N	N	
Print student's name	X	X	X	X	X	X	X	X	
Print marital status	X	X				X	X	X	
Print a "V"		X							
Print date of birth					X				
Print phone number				X					
Do not print									X

Fig. 3-12 Mixed-entry decision table for the student council listing.

table, where it will continue as instructed by the program.

Decision tables use the ELSE notation to take care of any combination of yes or no answers that have not been provided for in the condition entries. Figure 3-13 illustrates the use of all the fundamental notations used in decision tables.

Decision tables are used primarily to facilitate communications between management and systems professionals. Managers feel more at ease with the tables than with programming flowcharts. Decision tables are particularly useful for defining policy decisions in detail, presenting

Table 1 — Entry

If						
First record	Y					E
Salaried		Y				L
Eligible for O.T.			Y			S
Hourly				Y		E
Last record					Y	
Then						
Read a record	X					
Go to Table 2		X	X	X		
Do Table 5					X	
Write error message						X

Table 2 — Salary calculation

If		
Salaried	Y	Y
Hourly		Y
Eligible for O.T.	N	Y
Then		
Divide ann. sal. by 52	X	X
Mult. hrs. by rate		X
Subt. 35 from hrs. giving O.T. hrs.		X
Mult. O.T. hrs. by $1\frac{1}{2}$ rate		X
Add reg. + O.T. pay		X
Add gross pay to total	X	X X
Go to Table 3	X	X X

Table 3 — FICA calculation

If			
Ytd. gross $\geq$ \$13,200	Y	N	N
Ytd. gross + curr. sal. $\geq$ \$13,200		Y	N
Ytd. gross + curr. sal. $<$ \$13,200			Y
Then			
Multiply curr. sal. by FICA rate giving FICA tax			X
Subt. old ytd. gross from \$13,200 giving taxable income		X	
Multiply taxable income by FICA rate		X	
Go to Table 4	X	X	X

Table 4 — Deductions

If						
Union member	Y	Y	Y	N	N	
In retirement plan	Y	Y	N	Y	N	
Blue Cross member	Y	N	Y	Y	Y	
An employee	Y	Y	Y	Y	Y	N
Then						
Deduct union dues	X	X	X			
Deduct retirement cost	X	X		X		
Deduct BC-BS	X		X	X	X	
Deduct Fed. tax	X	X	X	X	X	
Deduct state tax	X	X	X	X	X	
Write an error message						X
Add net pay to total	X	X	X	X	X	

Table 5

Print out total of net pay	X
Print out total of gross pay	X
Stop run	X

Fig. 3-13 Simple payroll program illustrated in decision-table form.

program details to management for its approval, forcing both managers and programmers to think through the detailed conditions in a program, and communicating future management decisions that will require programming changes.

Study the underwriting chart of the Life Protection Society and answer these questions based on the information contained in the chart.

1. What would be the premium rate for a 23-year-old man in excellent health and in a Class 1 occupation?

2. What is the maximum amount of insurance that may be issued to a 46-year-old housewife (Class 1) in fair health?

3. What action would be taken on the application of a 63-year-old man in excellent health and in a Class 1 occupation?

4. What policy type would be issued to a 23-year-old housewife in excellent physical condition?

5. What is the premium rate for a 59-year-old man in fair health and in a Class 3 occupation?

GANTT CHARTING

The Gantt chart was the pioneer scheduling device. It is a simple bar chart that shows each event and its duration and is used primarily to compare the project's schedule with its actual progress. Ordinarily, the Gantt chart fails to show the relationship between one event and another.

Figure 3-14 illustrates a simple schedule for building a house. From it we can conclude that the construction is behind schedule, the house has not been sold, the garage has been started but is not finished, and the roof is still to be put on.

The Gantt chart has one important advantage over other display devices; it is simple. Managers are used to working with charts and in relatively simple projects they can comprehend a schedule and its status easily from a Gantt chart.

MINI-CASE 3.4

The master data card for the Last Chance Dating Service has the following format:

1–5   Customer Number
6–20   Customer Name
21   Sex

Life protection society – underwriting policy chart

																	ELSE
Age	<35	≥35 and <60	<35	≥35 and <60	<35	≥35 and <60	<35	≥35 and <60	<35	≥35 and <60	<35	≥35 and <60	<35	≥35 and <60	<35	≥35 and <60	
Sex	M	M	F	F	M	M	F	F	M	M	F	F	M	M	F	F	
Health	Ex	Ex	Ex	Ex	Fair	Fair	Fair	Fair	Ex	Ex	Ex	Ex	Fair	Fair	Fair	Fair	
Occupation Class	1	1	1	1	1	1	1	1	2	2	2	2	2	2	2	2	
Policy type	A	B	A	B	B	C	B	C	B	B	B	B	C	C	C	C	
Premium rate	0.28	1.47	0.21	1.22	1.51	1.91	1.27	1.86	0.28	1.28	0.26	1.26	0.95	2.12	1.45	2.01	
Maximum amt. of insurance	300,000	50,000	300,000	50,000	50,000	20,000	20,000	20,000	150,000	50,000	150,000	50,000	20,000	20,000	20,000	20,000	
Do not issue policy																	X

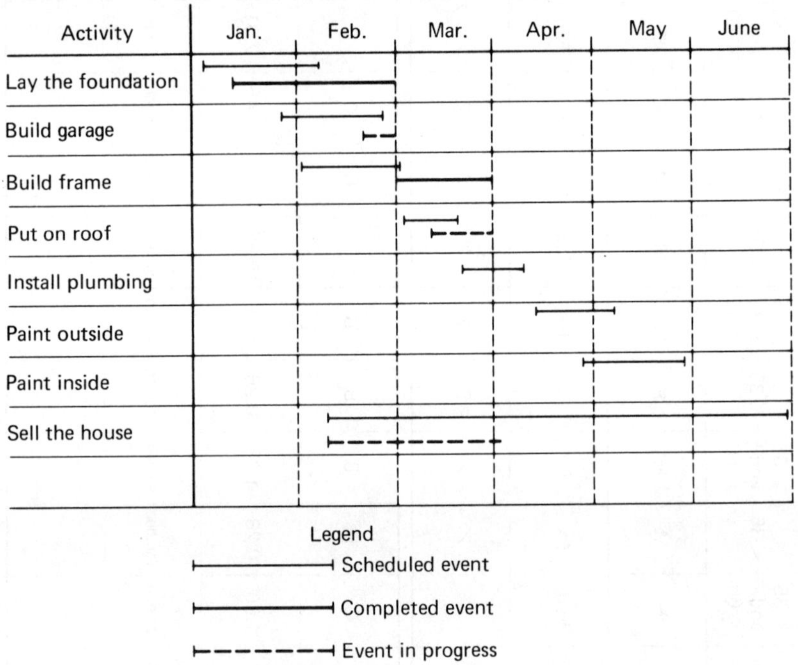

Fig. 3-14 Gantt chart for scheduling construction of a house.

	1 = male
	2 = female
22	Sex Appeal Code
	5 = super
	4 = very good looking
	3 = handsome or pretty
	2 = normal
	1 = mother loves him or her
23–28	Date of Birth
29	Marital Status
30–39	Phone Number
40–80	Other Statistical Data

Dolli Levi, the company's vice-president, has asked for a listing, in customer number order, of all single females in the file. Ms. Levi has also requested the following information on the list: the name and phone number for all single females in the file; the year of birth for those who are over 25 years of age; one asterisk to be printed after the name of anyone with a sex appeal code of 4 and two asterisks to be printed after the name for a sex appeal code of 5.

Write a decision table for this problem.

———————◆———————

glossary

block diagram   programming flowchart; diagram of the logical steps in a program

decision table   format for displaying the logic in a program in tabular form

extended entry   entry in a decision table in which the condition entries complete the questions contained in the condition stubs

limited-entry table   decision table which has only conditions that can be answered yes or no

mixed-entry table   decision table containing both limited and extended entries

programming flowchart   diagram of the logical steps in a program

systems flowchart   diagram of the steps in a system

REVIEW QUESTIONS

1. List five basic tools of the systems analyst.

2. State four guidelines to be observed in flowcharting.

3. What types of programs are particularly suitable for decision tables?

4. What are the uses of the basic tools of the systems analyst?

5. Distinguish between a systems flowchart and a programming flowchart.

6. What is the primary advantage of a Gantt chart?

7. What does charting a clerical system accomplish?

8. What are the primary purposes for flowcharting?

9. What advantages are there to using standard flowcharting symbols?

10. What are the symbols used for a programming flowchart?

11. What symbols are used for clerical flowcharting?

12. Express in decision table form the logical steps you would follow in deciding whether to buy a new car.

13. What names are given to the four quadrants in a decision table?

chapter 4

Basic Tools in
Systems Analysis: II

Objectives

In this chapter you will be introduced to the comparatively complex area of decision-making systems analysis tools.

The field of operations research uses mathematical and statistical models to simulate and solve business problems. Although the field of operations research is too complex to be treated in this first book of systems analysis, you should have an awareness of the potential of at least one of the methods used in operations research, linear programming. From doing the two sample problems in the text, you should become more aware of how the computer can be used as a business tool, and you can understand better the skill of the mathematical/statistical specialist of computer systems, the operations researcher.

The PERT chart is the standard device for scheduling complex projects. Even the simplest scheduling problem is displayed better through a PERT chart. You will be expected to know how to plot schedules on a PERT chart.

OPERATIONS RESEARCH

The computer originated as the tool of scientific decision making, performing in seconds or minutes mathematical calculations that previously took mathematicians months or years. Not surprisingly, its use has been extended to decision making in business. Operations research (OR) is the use of mathematical and statistical models to solve business problems.

A company's sophistication in data processing advances through two stages. In the first stage, the organization's basic accounting applications (payroll, receivables, payables, and inventory) are computerized. In the second stage, the computer generates the data needed by the organization for decision making. Initially, these data are in the form of printed reports, but eventually it is done through remote terminals. More sophisticated companies use operations research techniques such as linear programming and PERT scheduling to assist in making profitable decisions.

LINEAR PROGRAMMING

Models are often used as an aid to understanding and solving problems. For example, military leaders study mockups of significant battles to learn more about their strategic concepts; and aircraft designers judge the preliminary design of their airplanes by testing models in wind tunnels.

Similarly, models using mathematical symbols to represent real business situations can aid in solving business problems. The advantage of the mathematical model is that the calculating ability of the computer can be utilized to solve these problems.

Take, for example, the following two classic linear programming problems.

The Leahy Book Publishing Company publishes two monthly magazines, *Experience* and *Camp*. They are both produced on the same three machines; a printer, a collator, and a binder. These machines are also used for other, more profitable, printing at Leahy and are available to the magazine division on a limited basis. Their availability is:

Printer: 30 hr/month
Collator: 20 hr/month
Binder: 10 hr/month

Experience is a much larger magazine than *Camp* and requires more time for printing and collating. They require the same amount of time to be bound. Their production time per 1,000 copies is:

	Camp	Experience
Printer	2 hr	3 hr
Collator	1 hr	2 hr
Binder	1 hr	⅔ hr

Leahy's cost accountant reports that each 1,000 copies of *Experience* produces $100 in profits and 1,000 copies of *Camp* yields $70 in profits.

The manager of the magazines division wishes to know how many copies of each magazine he should produce each month to maximize profits.

The printer is available for 30 hours each month and requires 2 hours to print 1,000 copies (1 unit) of *Camp*. If the printer were used for these 30 hours to produce only *Camp*, it would print 15 units of the magazine.

If the allocated printer time were used exclusively for *Experience*, it would produce 10 units, or 10,000 copies.

These points of maximum production, 15 units for *Camp* and 10 units for *Experience*, are plotted on Fig. 4-1.

The line connecting these points represents the various combina-

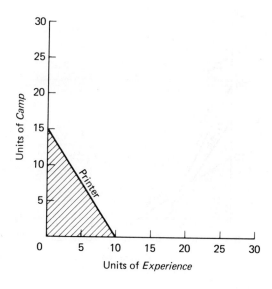

Figure 4-1

tions of *Camp* and *Experience* that can be produced by using the printer the full 30 hours. Any point in the shaded area represents a feasible production combination in which the printer is not used for the full 30 hours.

The production constraints imposed by the collator and binder may be plotted in the same manner (Fig. 4-2). If the collator's 20 hours were used exclusively for *Camp*, 20 units could be produced. If used for *Experience*, 10 units would be the maximum produced.

If the binder were used only for *Camp*, 10 units could be bound; if only *Experience* were produced, a maximum of 15 units could be bound.

The shaded area in Fig. 4-2 represents possible combinations of *Camp* and *Experience* that may be produced within the constraints imposed by the equipment. The lines *AB* and *BC* represent possible combinations of *Camp* and *Experience* that would maximize the use of the available time on the equipment. But the publisher wishes to know the combination that would be most profitable to the corporation. Thus the contribution-to-profit equation must be plotted to determine the optimum solution.

The systems analyst must define the constraints on production of the two magazines and express them in algebraic form. Examine these equations until you are convinced of their logic.

Printer Capacity:

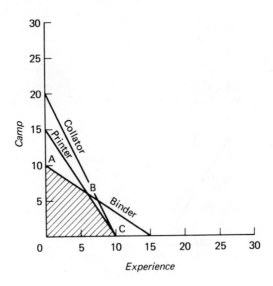

Figure 4-2

$$2 \ (Camp) + 3 \ (Experience) \leqq 30$$

Collator Capacity:

$$1 \ (Camp) + 2 \ (Experience) \leqq 20$$

Binder Capacity:

$$1 \ (Camp) + \tfrac{2}{3} \ (Experience) \leqq 10$$

The equation for printer capacity would read, "Two hours times the number of units of *Camp* to be printed plus 3 hours times the number of units of *Experience* to be printed must be less than or equal to 30 hours."

In addition to determining the equations for the constraints the equipment places on production, the systems analyst must define the relative profit each magazine makes. The following equation defines the contribution of each unit (1,000 copies of each magazine) to corporate profit:

$$\text{CONTRIBUTION} = 100 \ (Experience) + 70 \ (Camp)$$

Since this problem is relatively simple, containing only two products and three constraining machines, it may be solved graphically. Values for *Camp* are plotted on the y axis, and values for *Experience* are plotted on the x axis (Fig. 4-3).

To plot the contribution-to-profit line, any level of production is arbitrarily selected for one of the magazines. We chose 30 units of *Camp* as a level of production. Actually, 30 units can never be produced in a month because there is not sufficient machine capacity. If the theoretical production of 30 units of *Camp* were turned out, it would produce a profit of $2,100:

$$30 \text{ units} \times \$70 \text{ per unit} = \$2,100$$

To produce a profit of $2,100 publishing only *Experience,* 21 units of the magazine must be published:

$$\frac{\$2,100}{\$100 \text{ per unit}} = 21 \text{ units}$$

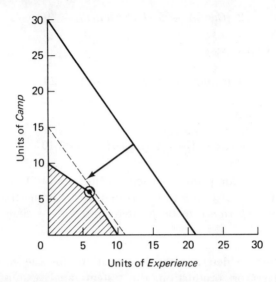

Figure 4-3

The relationship of contribution to profit for each magazine may be plotted. The two production points, 30 for *Camp* and 21 for *Experience,* are connected with a line. The line represents the combinations of *Experience* and *Camp* that may be produced to show a profit of $2,100. But machine restraints do not permit this many copies to be printed. To coordinate the machine restraints with the contribution-to-profits line of each magazine, the contribution line is advanced by parallel ruler to a place where it will intersect the machine constraints line. The first point of intersection will indicate the combination that will give the maximum profit. In the example given it is approximately 6 units of each magazine.

Obviously, a problem with 4 magazines and 12 machines could not be solved graphically. Solving the equations for this problem requires a computer.

The Fenton Mole Sporting Goods Company manufactures baseball bats at two factories. The bats are transported to each of two warehouses, from which they are distributed to retailers.

The plant in Doubleday produces 7,000 bats/day, the plant in Cobbsville manufactures 3,000. Demand for bats at the Eastern and Western warehouses is 5,000 each per day. It costs $100 to ship 1,000 bats from Doubleday to the Eastern warehouse, and $90 to the Western warehouse. To ship 1,000 bats from Cobbsville to Eastern costs $80, and from Cobbsville to Western costs $95. Graphically, the problem looks as shown in Fig. 4-4.

With a little thought, the solution to the problem is obvious. Doubleday has the greater capacity of the two plants and it ships bats $10 cheaper per thousand to Western than to Eastern. Thus, if it sent Western its full capacity of 5,000 bats, Western would require no shipment from Cobbsville. Cobbsville's full capacity of 3,000 bats would go to Eastern, which would receive the remaining 2,000 bats from Doubleday.

In practice, more variables usually exist. There could be 12 factories and 30 warehouses and the transportation among the various combinations may vary widely. The transportation problem must then be solved by computer program using the same logic we used to solve the simple program illustrated above.

To organize a solution to this problem, establish a matrix with the points of origin listed down the left side and the destinations across the top. The cost for each combination is written in a square in the upper

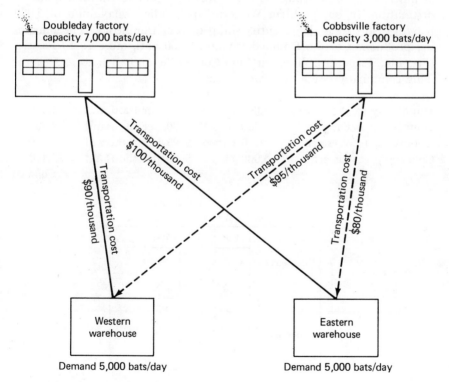

Figure 4-4

left hand corner of each space in the matrix (Fig. 4-5).

In this problem there are only four possible combinations for shipment between point of origin and destination, which we will call A, B, C, and D. The matrix is completed by putting in the column totals (demand) for each destination and the row totals for the capacity of each point of origin (Fig. 4-6).

Examine the illustration until you are convinced that these equations are valid:

$$A + B = 7,000$$

$$C + D = 3,000$$

$$A + C = 5,000$$

$$B + D = 5,000$$

An initial solution for the problem is formulated and tested for cost. The standard method for determining an initial solution is to ship as much as possible from the first point of origin to the first point of destination. In our problem Western can handle a maximum of 5,000 bats/day, so that is the quantity shipped from Doubleday. The remaining production of the Doubleday plant, 2,000 bats, must go to Eastern (Fig. 4-6). The entire shipment from Cobbsville must then go to Eastern. This combination (Fig. 4-7) would cost:

Doubleday to Western:	5,000 bats × $ 90 per thousand =	$4,500
Doubleday to Eastern:	2,000 bats × $100 per thousand =	2,000
Cobbsville to Western:	0 bats × $ 95 per thousand =	0
Cobbsville to Eastern:	3,000 bats × $ 80 per thousand =	$2,400
		$8,900

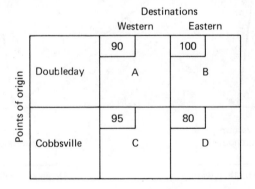

Figure 4-5

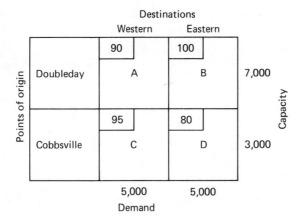

Figure 4-6

We know now that one possible solution to the problem would cost $8900, but the best solution is desired. To find it, each possible combination must be tested. Assuming that the bats are shipped in cartons of 1,000, we then change the quantity in the upper left sector of the matrix. This solution (Fig. 4-8) would be

$$
\begin{aligned}
4{,}000 \text{ bats} \times \$\ 90 \text{ per thousand} &= \$3{,}600 \\
3{,}000 \text{ bats} = \$100 \text{ per thousand} &= \ \ 3{,}000 \\
1{,}000 \text{ bats} \times \$\ 95 \text{ per thousand} &= \ \ \ \ \ 950 \\
2{,}000 \text{ bats} \times \$\ 80 \text{ per thousand} &= \ \ 1{,}600 \\
\hline
&\ \ \$9{,}150
\end{aligned}
$$

All possible solutions to the matrix must be tested similarly. It

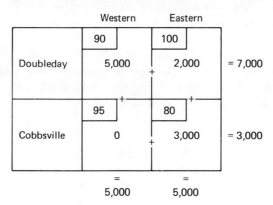

Fig. 4-7 Initial solution.

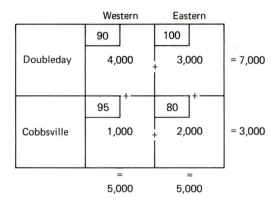

Fig. 4-8 Second feasible solution.

happens that in this problem the initial solution is the optimum one.

The value of this tool to the systems analyst is that the logic of the matrix and its arithmetic functions can be programmed so that far more involved matrices can be quickly solved. The systems analyst must define the origins, destinations, production capacities, demands, and transportation cost figures. He must understand the functions of the linear program and provide the program with accurate data.

It is possible to solve these problems through trial and error, taking each possible solution, testing it, and accepting the optimum solution. However, when the problem becomes more complex, as when there are 20 manufacturing sites and 10 warehouses, the reasonable capacity of a man to solve this problem has been exceeded. The systems analyst must turn to the various software programs available for solving generalized linear programming problems. Thus the role of the systems analyst is to define the variables and constraints involved in a problem in terms required by the particular program that he is using.

The production problem may serve as an example of the logic required for solving a linear programming problem. The illustration is simple enough to be solved with a graph, but more realistic problems require the use of a computer program.

PERT CHARTING

A PERT chart is a diagramming technique for planning and evaluating progress on complicated projects. Some projects have thousands of steps and some steps may not be started until others are completed.

The United States Navy, in cooperation with the management consulting firm of Booz, Allen and Hamilton developed PERT (Project Evaluation and Review Technique) to control the development of the Polaris atomic submarine. Today, PERT has wide acceptance in both military and commercial projects.

There are usually only two symbols in a PERT network: the circle, which is used for an event, or milestone, in a project, and the line, which represents the activity to be completed before the milestone is reached. Sometimes a rectangle is used to represent an event. Activities consume time; for our purposes, events are points in time that do not consume time.

A significant step in making up a PERT chart is determining which events are dependent upon others. Events that require the completion of one before the next may be started are serial; events that occur concurrently are parallel events.

In Fig. 4-9, where events 4, 3, and 2 are parallel, note that all three must occur before event number 1 can be reached. They are referred to as *predecessor events;* event 1 is a *successor event.*

Although it is not mandatory, it is customary to number events

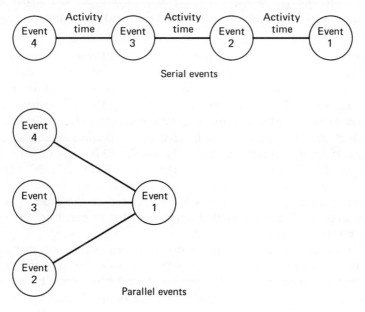

Events 4, 3, and 2 are in parallel; they do not depend on each other for their completion.

Fig. 4-9 Pert charting serial and parallel events.

from right to left. In this numbering system, event number 1 will be the completion of the job. Examine Fig. 4-10 and answer these questions.

1. The activity time between events 5 and 3 is how many days?
2. How long does event 4 take?
3. Between which two events is the longest activity time?
4. How long will it take from the time the play is cast until the show goes on?
5. If the play is to open on January 25, when must the decision be made as to which play is to be produced?

True–False

6. Event 6 is the predecessor event for event 7.
7. Events 5, 6, and 7 are parallel events.
8. Event 8 has no predecessor events.
9. Events 5, 3, and 2 are serial events.
10. Event 7 is a successor event to event 8.

ANSWERS: (1) 15 days (2) Events do not take time (3) 6 and 2 (4) 21 days (5) January 1 (6) False (7) True (8) True (9) True (10) True

If you correctly answered questions 9 and 10, you can see some of the advantages of PERT charting. In question 9 it took 20 days from casting time until the dress rehearsal, and one more day before the performance. A director, analyzing this chart, would easily realize that if the show is to be produced on a certain date, he better have his cast selected 21 days before, or he will have to cut corners somewhere.

Question 10 illustrates another use of the PERT chart. The chart reveals several different paths from the time of the original decision until the play is performed. Since the play cannot go on until all the steps are complete, the director will recognize that the most time-consuming steps are from events 8 through 6 and 2 to event 1: this is the chart's critical path.

The chart also indicates two paths in which spare time exists (Fig. 4-11). Whereas the critical path takes 25 days from event 8 to event 1, the path from event 8 through events 5, 3, and 2 to event 1 only takes 21 days, and the path from event 8 through events 7 and 4 to 1 takes 11 days. These paths with spare time are known as slack paths.

PERT charts are usually constructed starting with the first event, but they may be started with the last. The selection of a specific method is largely a matter of style.

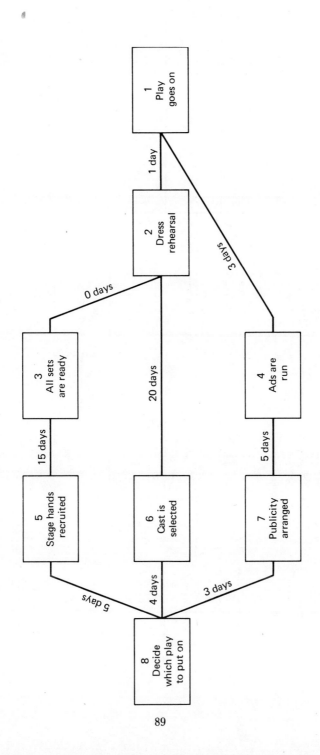

Fig. 4-10 Pert chart for scheduling a play.

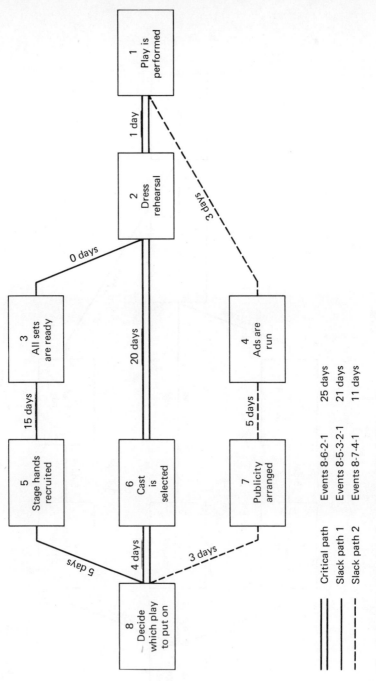

Fig. 4-11 Critical and slack paths for scheduling a play.

Within the figure:

1 Play is performed

2 Dress rehearsal

3 All sets are ready

4 Ads are run

5 Stage hands recruited

6 Cast is selected

7 Publicity arranged

8 Decide which play to put on

1 day

3 days

0 days

20 days

15 days

5 days

5 days

4 days

3 days

Critical path   Events 8-6-2-1   25 days
Slack path 1   Events 8-5-3-2-1   21 days
Slack path 2   Events 8-7-4-1   11 days

Estimating Activity Time

To produce a PERT network, the project planner must determine and list each step in the project. This in itself is an extensive task but even more difficult is estimating the time for each step. In the example of putting on a play, you may question that it takes 20 days from the time the play is cast until the dress rehearsal was determined. Quite possibly, some directors will estimate 30 days; others 10.

The systems analyst must find the best estimates available for each activity in a PERT chart. These estimates may come from someone on an assembly line, an experienced supervisor, or perhaps a professional estimator. Accurate estimating is a rare skill. The inexperienced tend to underestimate.

It is unreasonable to expect even the best estimators to be perfectly correct in all their estimates. For this reason, statisticians have developed a formula for determining the expected activity time:

$$t_e = \frac{t_o + 4t_m + t_p}{6}$$

where

t_e = expected activity time

t_o = optimistic estimate; there is only 1 chance in 100 the activity can be completed in that time

t_m = most likely completion time

t_p = pessimistic estimate, there is only 1 chance in 100 that the activity will take this long

An estimator says: "I think the job most likely will be completed in 9 days. If things go poorly, we could take up to 21 days to get it done. If everything falls into place, we'll wrap it up in 3 days." How long will the estimated activity time be?

$$t_o = 3$$
$$t_m = 9 \qquad \frac{3 + 36 + 21}{6} = 10 \text{ days}$$
$$t_p = 21$$

estimated activity time = 10 days

Estimated time is often given in weeks and tenths of a week. People have found this particularly convenient since a half-day is equal to a tenth of a week.

MINI-CASE 4.1

Examine Fig. 4-12 and determine the t_e for each activity time. Activity time is usually identified by its predecessor and successor events. Fill in the activity time in the chart.

Event	t_o	t_m	t_p	t_e
12-11	1	3	11	4
11-10				
11- 9				
10- 8				
10- 5				
9- 7				
9- 3				
8- 4				
7- 1				
6- 2				
5- 2				
4- 2				
3- 1				
2- 1				

By looking at the chart, can you determine the critical path?

Which are the slack paths?

What is the fastest time in which the entire job can be completed?

Perhaps you were able to figure out the answers to the questions by merely looking at the chart, but as a project becomes more complex, one's quick judgment can be deceiving. The critical path can be determined through manual calculations in small networks, that is, networks with perhaps less than 100 steps in them. When a network is more complex, a computer is used.

Calculating Paths Manually

To calculate the slack and critical paths on a PERT network, two factors must be determined for each event:

TE—the earliest date an event may be completed

TL—the latest possible date an event may be completed without delaying the project

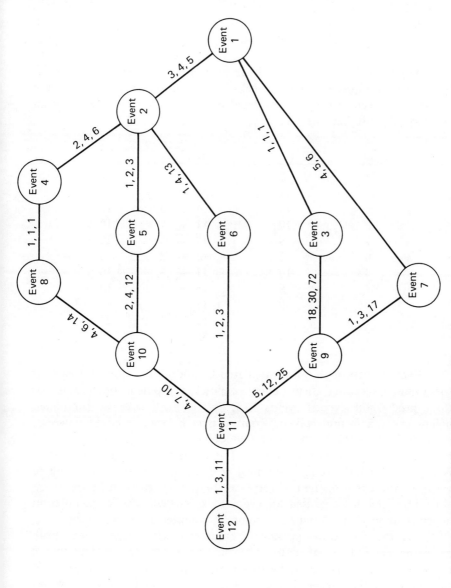

Fig. 4-12 Sample pert chart (all estimates are in whole weeks).

93

In Fig. 4-13 the *TE* for each event has been calculated. Trace these calculations through.

To calculate *TE*, start by assigning the first event, in this case event 12, the starting time 0. The earliest that event 11 can take place is 4 weeks after the starting time of the project, so its *TE* is 4. Event 10 can be completed 11 days after the beginning of the project at the earliest.

Try event 7. It takes 4 weeks from event 12 to event 11, 13 weeks from event 11 to event 9, and 5 weeks from event 9 to event 7. Thus the earliest that event 7 can be completed is in 22 weeks. The *TE* for each event is calculated as follows:

Event	Predecessor	Calculation	*TE*
11	12	4	4
10	11	4 + 7	11
9	11	4 + 13	17
8	10	11 + 7	18
7	9	17 + 5	22
6	11	4 + 2	6
5	10	11 + 5	16
4	8	18 + 1	19
3	9	17 + 35	52
2	4	19 + 4	23
1	3	52 + 1	53

Events 11 through 3 are calculated by adding the times for each of the events preceding them. Event 2 poses a problem because it has three predecessor events; events 4, 5, and 6. Each must be completed before event 2 is undertaken. Event 6 may be completed in 6 weeks; event 5, in 16 weeks. The event that determines the earliest date that event 2 can be performed is event 4. The earliest that event 4 is possible is 19 weeks after the start of the project. Since it takes 4 weeks to get to event 2 from event 4, the earliest 2 can be performed is in 23 weeks.

The same logic is used for event 1. Its earliest possible completion depends upon event 3, which cannot be completed for 52 weeks.

TL, the latest an event may be completed without the entire project being delayed, is calculated by assigning a completion date to the final event and working backwards to the first event. In our problem we know that the earliest the project can be completed is in 53 weeks. Moreover, if event 1 is not completed in 53 weeks, the entire project will be behind schedule. The *TE* and the *TL* for the last event are always the same.

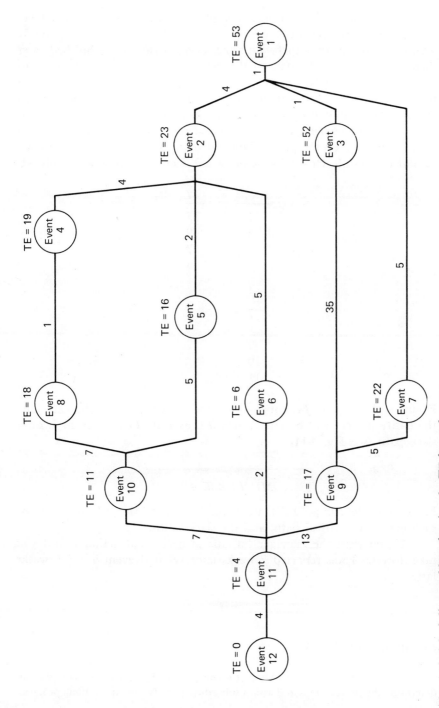

Fig. 4-13 Scheduling problem showing the TE for each event.

If the latest event 1 can be completed is in 53 weeks, and it takes 1 week to go from event 3 to event 1, the TL for event 3 must be 52 weeks. For the project to be on time, event 3 cannot be finished later than 52 weeks from the start of the project. Notice, however, that event 2 can be finished as late as 49 weeks from the start without delaying the project. Its TE is 23 and its TL is 49. Since it can possibly be finished in 23 weeks, but it need not be completed in 49 weeks, the event has slack time. Ask yourself what is the latest each event may be completed without holding up the project, and calculate the TL for each event. Be careful of event 9. How long before event 3 must event 9 be completed?

Event	TL
1	53
2	49
3	52
4	45
5	
6	
7	
8	
9	
10	
11	

Events with TL and TE equal lie on the critical path. If they are late, the entire project will be late. When TL exceeds TE, the event is on a slack path (see Fig. 4-14).

MINI-CASE 4.2

Figure 4-15 depicts a PERT network. Determine the TL and TE for each event, the critical path, and the slack paths.

If you were the manager for this project, what action would you take if event 3 was reported 2 weeks late? What if event 5 was 4 weeks late?

Advantages of PERT

highlights key steps—After studying the PERT chart, a manager can determine the critical steps and assign subordinates to follow up on their progress.

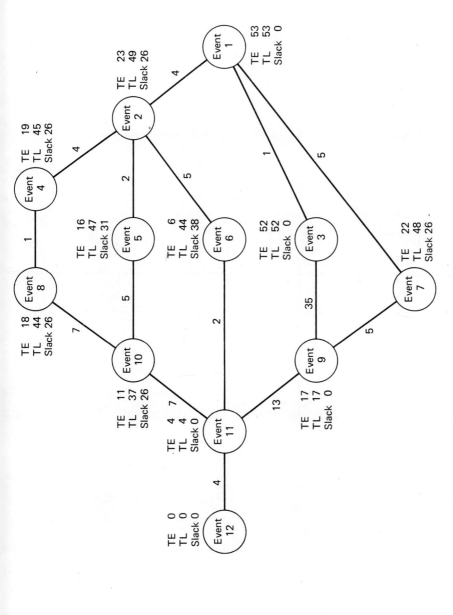

Fig. 4-14 Scheduling problem showing TE, TL, and slack time for each event.

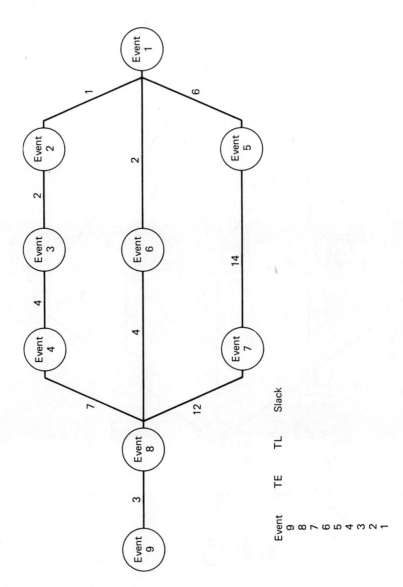

Event	TE	TL	Slack
9			
8			
7			
6			
5			
4			
3			
2			
1			

Figure 4-15

allows progress assessment and control—If a critical step is behind schedule, the manager may choose to use more of his staff on that aspect of the problem, or he may use overtime. Conversely, a manager can avoid wasting his human and financial resources in expediting steps that have little effect on the completion date.

flexibility—PERT charts are dynamic; they can be altered to meet changing needs while a project is in progress.

requires thoughtful planning—PERT charting requires the manager to think through each step in a project and to analyze the relationship of each step to the others in the project.

PERT is a business tool, not a panacea. Managers can plan and control projects better when using this technique, but PERT is certainly not a substitute for good management.

• *GROUP PROBLEM 4.1* •

The L. David Lloyd Corporation manufactures children's clothing. Lloyd's Clothing has factories in Fall River, Massachusetts, and Providence, Rhode Island. Its business office is located in Providence.

Four weeks ago, the management of L. David Lloyd, Inc., ordered an IBM 360/20 computer due in 40 weeks, to handle its inventory, receivables, and management information reporting. L. David Lloyd has produced management reports manually until now.

Yesterday, you received a memo stating that you have been selected as the coordinator of the computer installation. Specifically, you are responsible for site preparation, staffing, training, systems development, and program writing. Moreover, management wants a report of your plans by the end of the week.

You took a preliminary survey of the opinions currently held by management at L. David Lloyd's. Your conclusions:

1. Management anticipates that the computer will be located at the business office in Providence. No further plans have been made for site preparation.

2. Management feels that it requires some outside professional help to develop its computer systems. It is not certain how much help it requires.

3. Management wants "something" operating when the computer is plugged in. It feels that the computer can reduce costs within 1 year of installation.

4. The company has a policy of promotion from within that it hopes to follow as much as possible in staffing for the computer.

5. Your inquiries around the company indicate that you know as much about installing a computer as anyone else in the company.

6. L. David Lloyd's currently employs 463 people, mostly in production.

Present your plan for organizing L. David Lloyd's computer installation in no more than two typewritten pages. Document your plans with whatever displays and charts you feel are necessary.

glossary

activity time   time between events in a PERT network

critical path   those events in a PERT network which, if behind schedule, will cause the final event in the network to be late

event   point in time in a PERT network; a milestone

linear programming   problem-solving technique that uses mathematical formulas to solve business problems on a computer

milestone   event in a system that is used to measure and evaluate progress

model   system expressed in mathematical terms

OR   Operations Research: a general term for the use of scientific tools to solve business problems

PERT   Project Evaluation and Review Technique; a project scheduling and control technique

slack path   events in a PERT network in which some spare time exists before they must be completed

REVIEW QUESTIONS

1. What is the role of the systems analyst in linear programming?

2. What are the advantages of a PERT chart over a Gantt chart? What are the disadvantages?

3. Would scientific decision making have developed without the computer?

4. Explain how time estimates are calculated for a PERT chart.

5. What are the chances that an optimistic estimate will actually occur?

6. Why are time estimates often given in weeks and tenths of weeks?

7. Identify each of the following: T_o, T_m, T_p, T_e, TE, and TL.

8. Identify the two principal stages through which a company advances as it gains sophistication in data processing.

9. Give three instances where modeling is used in decision making.

10. How was PERT charting developed?

11. What is the difference between events and activities in a PERT chart?

12. What is the difference between serial and parallel events in a PERT chart?

13. What is meant by the phrase "PERT charts are dynamic."

14. The Ballou Manufacturing Company produces two finished goods: product 20 and product 21. They are produced on the same three machines, A, B, and C. Each month these machines are available for manufacturing product 20 and product 21 as follows:

Machine A	20 hours
Machine B	35 hours
Machine C	15 hours

Each unit of product 20 and product 21 requires the following machine time:

	Product 20	Product 21
Machine A	3 hr	4 hr
Machine B	2 hr	3 hr
Machine C	2 hr	1 hr

If each unit of product 20 contributes $50 to profit and each unit of product 21 contributes $75 to profit, how many units of each product should be produced each month to maximize profits?

chapter 5

Forms Design

Objectives

Forms design is another tool that the systems analyst must master. You will learn the essentials for designing input forms for recording data and output forms for displaying it.

There are many techniques in forms design, which although simple, can greatly improve the efficiency of a system. You will design punched card and multiple-part forms as well as forms used with various input/output devices. One special type of form, the turnaround document, which is completed by the customer, will be given special attention because of its importance in computer systems.

Design factors in hardware often limit the potential of computer input/ output devices. Too often, systems analysts design forms that restrict them even further. A form is essentially a document with two components: preprinting, and blanks for inserting data. In electronic data processing, we deal with forms that create accurate and efficient input to a computer system, as well as forms that display computer output.

Well-designed forms serve four purposes: to control work flow, to reduce redundancies in recording data, to increase clerical accuracy, and to allow easier checking of data.

DESIGNING INPUT FORMS

Input forms generally have preprinted information and spaces to be filled in by a person. The data are then converted to machine-readable form by a key-driven device. Therefore, one has three primary concerns when designing input documents: the person filling out the form, the key machine operator, and the device that reads the data into the computer. All three are vital to the computer system, but the requirements of each vary with the hardware available.

Consider a third-generation computer capable of handling punched card and magnetic tape input. Such computers have tremendous potential for sorting large amounts of data, and obviously can rearrange data faster than a human. As long as there is a sufficient number of transactions in the system, there is no need to arrange the data in a form to suit the computer, because a computer can reformat data itself with a comparatively simple program. Therefore, as forms designers, we concern ourselves primarily with the people in the system.

The keypunch operator must receive the data in a form that can be readily understood. Whenever possible, source documents to be keypunched should be designed so that the keypunch operator can punch the card as he reads the source document—left to right, top to bottom. Ideally, the form should be designed so that the person completing it can do so conveniently. The keypunch operator should punch the data in the order it is on the form, and the computer should reformat it when required.

The following is a checklist for designing input documents:

1. What sources are used by the person using the form?
2. What can be preprinted on the form to reduce coding and keypunch errors?
3. What other functions does the form perform in addition to providing computer input?
4. What size form is appropriate and convenient for the data?
5. What type of paper is most appropriate?

6. What techniques of forms design can be used to make the clerical process speedier and more accurate?

7. What spacing, margins, typeface, headings, and lines are needed for the form?

Who fills out computer input forms? The person who prepares input data is usually from the clerical staff of an organization, but this generalization is not always true. Often, a form is filled out by a customer, as in bank deposits and many types of address changes. In these cases the data come from the person completing the form and it is reasonable to concentrate on arranging the data on the form for the keypunch operator as long as the customer is not confused by the format. However, a clerk in a business organization may find that the data come from several sources; therefore, the input form should be suited to these sources as much as possible, rather than to the needs of the keypunch operator or the computer.

Probably the simplest form to consider is the coding sheet (Fig. 5-1). The coding sheet is a document designed to record data specifically for entry into a data system through keyed input. It is used primarily when the data to be assembled come from a variety of sources and must be consolidated into one input record before reaching the computer. When designing a coding sheet, three priorities for placement of data should be kept in mind:

1. To enable the coder to work as quickly and as accurately as possible

2. To enable the keypunch operator to punch the data from left to right and from top to bottom

3. The format should be geared for the computer program only when the volume of transactions is too small to justify computer sorting.

In designing any form, the designer must consider whether or not the form will be completed by handwriting or mechanical device. Each form should be designed so that the data will enter the system in the correct format. For handwritten documents, space should be allowed only for the maximum number of characters that each field can contain (see Figs. 5-2 and 5-3). The form should force the coder into clerical accuracy whenever possible. When the coder is given a choice, he may code a name with 21 characters where the system will only accept 18.

A coding sheet can be a source of information to anyone who must supply data for it. Rather than have a coder look up a coding structure in a manual, one can save him time and improve clerical accuracy by printing the coding structure on the form (Fig. 5-4).

Most forms, however, serve other functions besides being the input media for a computer system. For example, an application for a life insur-

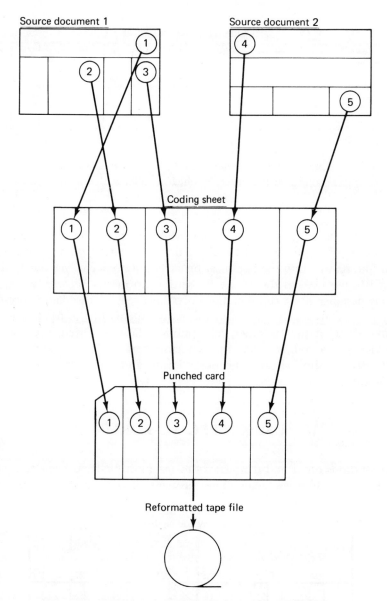

Fig. 5-1 When there is heavy volume, the coding sheet and the
punched card should be designed so that the coder and
the keypunch operator can pick up the information from
left to right, starting at the top of the form. As long as
the computer has tape or disk capabilities it can reformat the data.

Address record coding sheet

Name (first name first)	Street Address	City	State	Zip	Blank
1 20	21 44	45 56	57 68	69 73	

Fig. 5-2 A coding sheet for address records. Note that the data are arranged in the order in which a coder will usually find it.

ance policy is a legal document that, when accepted, binds the company to insure the applicant's life. Not all the information on an application will find its way into the organization's computer system; yet the application is often used as the source for setting up master records. Here, the forms designer must consider not only the needs of the data processing system, but also such matters as the requirements of the legal staff, the convenience of the customer, and public relations. Often, the primary contact that a company has with its customers is through applications, bills, deposit slips, checks, and other forms, and these forms then determine the company's public image.

USING SPECIAL FORMS

Corporations often find it necessary to use multiple-part forms to accomplish specific business goals. The payment of one of the corporation's

Salary survey coding sheet

Social security number	Skip	Annual salary	Skip	Code
1 3 4 5 6 9		21 27		80

Fig. 5-3 Coding sheet designed to be completed by hand. Note how the form is designed to force the coder to put the correct amount of digits in each field. Note, too, the use of the dotted line to separate the dollars from the cents.

debts may require one copy for the file, another for the auditor, and a third for the accounting department, which must produce the check. Legal requirements sometimes dictate the use of a multiple-part form. For example, the W-2 form is required to report the employee's earnings to the federal government, the employee, and the state.

Multiple-part forms can generally be classified as vendor-manufactured or internally made. The vendor-manufactured type is made with perforations so that the form can be torn apart to separate the original and the various parts of the form from the carbons. Internally made forms are limited by the facilities of the duplicating department of the organization. Probably the simplest type of internally made form is produced by making a pad of perhaps 50 or 100 copies of the form. Whenever more than one copy is required, the person completing the form has only to insert the desired number of carbons and fill in the data.

On occasion, all the information on the original form is not required on the copies. For instance, an accounting transaction may require an original signature on every copy of a voucher, but the remaining information may be carbons. For situations such as this, a form may be designed with a partial carbon inserted so that a signature on the original will not come through on the copies. Multiple-part forms become expensive, as the cost increases rapidly as more nonroutine techniques are used. In fact, whenever a form requires the use of an outside shop instead of the organization's own printing facilities, substantial increases in cost

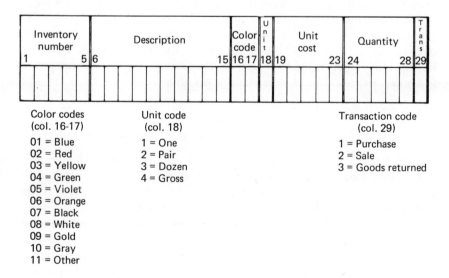

Inventory number	Description	Color code	Unit	Unit cost	Quantity	Trans
1 5	6 15	16 17	18	19 23	24 28	29

Color codes (col. 16-17)	Unit code (col. 18)	Transaction code (col. 29)
01 = Blue	1 = One	1 = Purchase
02 = Red	2 = Pair	2 = Sale
03 = Yellow	3 = Dozen	3 = Goods returned
04 = Green	4 = Gross	
05 = Violet		
06 = Orange		
07 = Black		
08 = White		
09 = Gold		
10 = Gray		
11 = Other		

Fig. 5-4 When coding structures are detailed on a form, clerical accuracy will increase.

usually occur.

However, in weighing the production costs of all forms, the direct cost must always be balanced against the clerical time required and the increased possibility of error when the documents are processed individually.

In analyzing the use of multiple-part forms, the systems analyst should cultivate a skeptical attitude. Departments in business organizations tend to want their own copy of everything, even when it is not necessary. The more centralized and computer-oriented a system is, the less is the need for additional parts of a form.

The size of a form is a significant factor in its design. Since the standard-sized sheet of paper is 8½ by 11 inches, this size, or one half or one third of it, is the most economical to use in designing forms. Other factors, such as where the form will be stored after it is processed, or whether or not the form will be inserted into an envelope, often justify using nonstandard paper sizes. The principle is to design a form that meets the requirements of the overall system.

The paper used for the form should always be a consideration. A form that is frequently handled needs a sturdier stock than one that is used once. Forms that have a public relations value, such as a bill or a contract, should be produced on a better stock.

Sometimes the system requires that the form be printed on a punched card. Public utilities, for example, often send their bills in punched card form. Sometimes the customer is asked to write the amount of his remittance on the face of the card. These data, along with other prepunched information, such as account number, serve as input to the data processing system. The concept of sending a form to the customer, having him return it, and using that form in the data processing system is known as turnaround document processing.

DESIGNING OUTPUT DOCUMENTS

The primary consideration in output document design is to arrange the data in a form most convenient to the user. Of course, the format is limited by the specifications of the output device that produces it.

For years, the high-speed printer has been the standard device for producing output forms, but today computer programmers and systems analysts can also work with such output hardware as teleprocessing terminals, cathode ray tubes, and microfilm. However, the forms-design principles remain constant despite the use of new media.

In dealing with output, we must return to the basic elements of a form: preprinted information and spaces to be filled in by the user. In the case of output forms, the computer fills out the form. The preprinted portion of the form may literally be preprinted by a forms vendor, or it may be produced as page and column headings by the computer program. One expects computer programmers to have a fairly good concept of how to display computer output so that users readily understand it. Since the computer can store and print descriptive information as well as data, an important task of both the systems analyst and the programmer is to determine which preprinted or repetitive information should be provided on each page of printed output or each visual display of output.

Since the printer is still the most widely used of the output devices, we will concentrate on it in this section. Remember that output forms for a computer printer are continuous forms that are separated from each other by a perforated line. They may be single sheets, multiple-part forms with carbon interleaved, or multiple-part NCR forms. NCR forms are printed on chemically treated paper and make copies without the use of carbon. Continuous-form punched cards are available for use when the output form will eventually reenter the system as data input.

Each computer printer has its own specifications for producing output. For example, most printers can print either 6 or 8 lines vertically to an inch, with six being the standard. Most computers also have a standard of 10 characters to an inch for horizontal spacing, and can usually print over 100 characters on a line. We will use the specifications of the IBM 1403N printer here. It prints 10 characters to an inch and 132 characters to a line horizontally. Vertical spacing is either 6 or 8 lines to an inch.

Precision is vital in designing output forms. Of course, the preprinted data can be printed to virtually any specifications, but it must be planned to coincide with the data the computer will produce.

Try this problem in designing an output form.

MINI-CASE 5.1

The Life Protection Society of the United States is a small life insurance company located in Hartford, Connecticut. Until recently most of its paperwork operations have been performed manually by a large clerical staff, but the installation of a third-generation computer 6 months ago is bringing about systems changes. The computer configuration consists of a card reader, a card punch, four tape drives, two disk packs, and an IBM 1403N high-speed printer.

You have been asked to design one of the output forms in the system for processing life insurance policies. Each month, Life Protection produces a cross-reference list of its policyholders for internal use. The list contains:

Policy Number	8 digits
Insured's Name	18 letters
Other Policies Owned by Insured	8 digits (there can be as many as 10 for each policyholder)
Social Security Number	9 digits

Design the output format for this listing.

The following is a checklist for designing output documents:

1. Should the headings on the form be produced by the computer printer or by a vendor?

2. Precisely what header information should appear at the top of each page?

3. What terminology should be used for the column headings to make the meaning of the data clear?

4. Are the column spacings planned so that they can be easily read?

5. What preprinted instructions on the form would be helpful?

6. Has the form been designed to meet the requirements of the printer being used?

7. How is the form used after it is produced? Is it microfilmed? Stored in a binder? Is the form separated or kept intact?

MULTIPLE-PART OUTPUT FORMS

Most forms used by computer printers are continuous forms produced by a vendor. A vendor can supply as many copies of a form as a printer can handle, but when more than an original and one copy of a form is required, the forms designer should be cautious. Some printers encounter trouble when a form has more than four parts to it, but this is only part of the problem. Multiple-part forms must have the carbon decolated and often the forms must be separated before distribution. These time-consuming and expensive procedures should be avoided whenever possible. The real cost of multiple-part forms occurs when they are distributed and many additional people become involved in their handling. The benefits a corporation derives from these extra copies of a form must offset these additional costs.

It is necessary sometimes to produce several hundred copies of a form printed on a computer. Of course, the forms may be photocopied, but this is expensive. Another solution is to produce the report on a continuous-form stencil and have an inexpensive duplicating machine run off the necessary copies.

DESIGNING A TURNAROUND DOCUMENT

The turnaround document requires skillful design because it must fit into so many aspects of the system. Often, it is originally output from a computer printer and must meet the printer's specifications. Since it is often sent to the customer in an envelope, it must fit the envelope; and if the document contains the name and address of the customer, the location of these data must match the positioning of the envelope window.

Next, the needs of the customer must be satisfied. Whatever instructions he needs to complete the form correctly must be given. Unless the form is designed so that the customer will indeed fill it out correctly and return it to the company, the purpose of the turnaround document has been defeated. Finally, the forms designer must consider how the form will be used when it returns to the company. He must consider how the form is processed, who processes it, how the form relates to the hardware available, and how it relates to associated systems in the company.

The following is a checklist for designing turnaround documents:

1. Can the document be produced on a standard computer printer?

2. Will the document be mailed in a closed or a window envelope?

3. If a window envelope is used, will the printing of the name and address be spaced to show through the window?

4. What instructions must be printed on the form to ensure that the customer will remit the correct amount and return it to the company?

5. Will you enclose an envelope for return mailing?

6. Will you use a punched card for the document? If so, what problems will you encounter with the hardware available?

7. Consider how you will process the return document.

8. Should you make provision for the customer to provide additional information, such as name and address?

9. Have you included spaces for all data that must be completed on the form?

10. Is this form an important part of the public relations or "image" of the company?

11. Should the form be printed in black ink or are other colors needed?

12. Is the form laid out so that the customer can easily see where to put the information?

MINI-CASE 5.2

The Life Protection Society of the United States sends a dividend check to each of its policyholders once a year on the anniversary of the issuance of the policy. The computer calculates the amount of the dividend for those customers who will be receiving a check in a given month and writes out a complete tape record to be used for checkwriting. We have been asked to design the dividend check.

SAMPLE SOLUTION TO MINI-CASE 5.2

As we start the problem, we know the following: The data to be printed on the check are available on magnetic tape. Some further investigation reveals that the management wants the policy number, the check number, the amount of the dividend, the current date, and the policyholder's name and address printed on the check. The signature authorizing the check will be printed by a check-signing machine after the check has been printed. The Life Protection Society has an IBM 1403N high-speed printer.

The first step is to decide whether the check will be produced on paper or on a punched card. We will select the punched card because it is more suitable as a turnaround document. (A check eventually comes back to the company for the reconciliation process.) Moreover, we know that we can print checks on continuous-form punched cards as easily as we can on paper.

The checks could be mailed in a sealed envelope with a typed address or with sticky-back address labels produced on the computer printer. Both these possibilities create extra work. The name and address are on the check-writing tape; therefore, we can print the name and address of the policyholder to show through the envelope window. So we must design two forms: a check and an envelope with a window located to match the check.

Since the check will be a punched card, the size of the form is predetermined. The standard punched card is $7\frac{3}{8}$ by $3\frac{1}{4}$ inches. The basic definition of a form specifies that it contains two elements: preprinted information and spaces to be filled in with data. We now must decide which information can be preprinted and which must be filled in, in this case by the computer. Here, the following analysis should hold:

Check number	preprinted
Name and address of the company	preprinted
Name and address of the bank	preprinted
Payee's name	data
Payee's address	data
Amount of the check	data
Date of the check	data
Authorized signature	*
Policy number	data

In general, information that is common to every check and will be exactly the same on each check can be preprinted. In the case of a check, the following analysis is valid.

The preprinted information can be positioned by a forms vendor practically anywhere we require it. The limitations on positioning the printing on this form are imposed by the computer printer. Life Protection's IBM 1403 printer prints 10 characters to an inch horizontally, and 6 lines to an inch vertically. Figure 5-5 illustrates a form designed to these specifications.

There is an important additional consideration in designing checks. We mentioned that the check is a turnaround document because it is returned to the company and becomes input to the check reconciliation process, but it is also an input document to the bank's accounting system. Before the check's design can be finalized, the bank's systems people must be consulted. Most banks use magnetic ink coding for sorting checks; therefore, this coding must be incorporated into the check's design. Again, we come back to the principle that a form must serve an entire system.

Examine the sample form carefully. Use a ruler to check the vertical and horizontal spacing. If you were designing the form, what changes would you incorporate to make it more functional, more appealing?

* Although the authorized signature is not data, it cannot be preprinted, for security reasons.

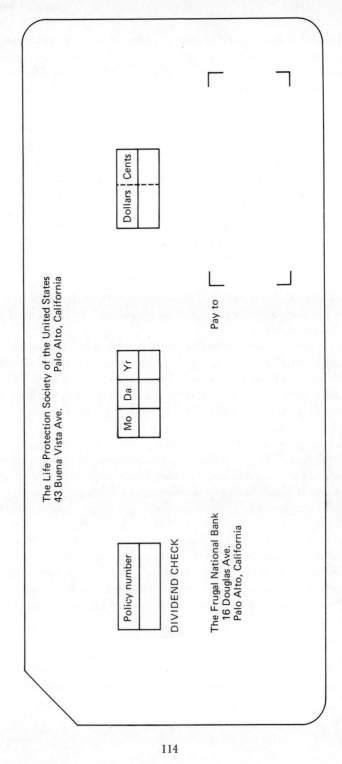

Fig. 5-5 Possible solution to Mini-Case 5.2.

DESIGNING PUNCHED CARDS

People often associate punched cards with their function of introducing data into a computer. However, punched cards can serve other functions, as in the case of the Life Protection Society's dividend check. For instance, when a coder writes input data directly on a card, the card serves as a source document. Using a card this way has several limitations. First, not all of the card is visible to the keypunch operator while he is punching. Figure 5-6 illustrates the area on the card that is obscured by the machine's punching mechanism during operation. When designing cards that will be used as coding documents, one must coordinate the location of the field to be punched with the location of the source data on the card. As a general rule, never put the source data in the same area on the cards where they are to be punched.

Some systems still use punched cards as master files. When such a system requires manual reference, for example, pulling an address card from the file for insertion of a change of address, the designer must be careful in arranging the displayed data. Data may be printed on a card by either a keypunch machine or an interpreter. The keypunch machine prints the data simultaneously with punching them, eliminating the extra step of interpretation. However, printing from a keypunch machine is often difficult to read, since all 80 characters in the card are crowded into one line. A card interpreter makes the characters easier to read since it only puts 60 on a line and gives considerable flexibility for arranging the data. However, interpretation requires an extra step after keypunching.

The primary consideration when designing cards is the location of the fields to be punched. First, data should be punched in the same order in which they are read. Second, if there are several cards in a system and some of them contain the same fields, the common fields should have the same location on each card. Finally, cards for the same installation should be standardized as much as possible. Name fields should be standardized at a maximum of 18 or 20 positions and have a set format such as first name, middle initial, and last name.

SOME ELEMENTARY TECHNIQUES
IN FORMS DESIGN

One of the objectives of forms design is to increase the accuracy of input data. The following techniques in forms design may help to achieve this objective.

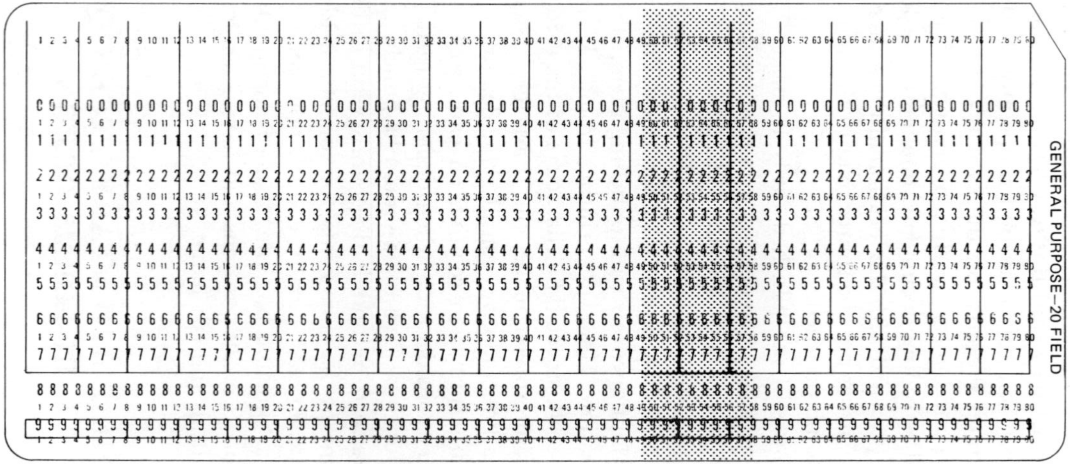

GENERAL PURPOSE—20 FIELD

Fig. 5-6 The shaded area indicates that part of the card which would be obscured when the operator is punching column 25. Ordinarily nine columns of a card are obscured while punching with an IBM 024 or 026. Other keypunch devices have different specifications.

116

box style

Boxing in each portion of a form makes it more attractive and can increase accuracy. Each space for filling in data is designed to make the coder put in only the desired amount of data. Examine Fig. 5-7 to see how each element of data is boxed off to assist the coder in completing the form.

shading

When one area is to be emphasized, it helps to shade that location. Shading is also used when a part of the form is not to be completed by the coder. When this technique is used, the instruction DO NOT WRITE IN THE SHADED AREA is printed clearly on the form.

check box

The check box is a technique for improving coding accuracy. It is especially effective when the form is being completed by a customer or the public. People are more apt to check off a box than fill in a space. Look at the contrasting styles in Fig. 5-8.

colors

Contrasting colors give emphasis to areas on a form. A different colored ink is often used to print the instructions on a form.

MINI-CASE 5.3

The Life Protection Society of the United States is automating its premium-billing operation, and you are the assistant systems analyst on the project. Until now, premium notices have been prepared on EAM equipment, but a new system is being developed to produce these notices on the IBM 1403N printer. Life Protection currently has 83,000 premium-paying policyholders. They remit premiums on the following schedule:

Monthly	78%
Quarterly	8%
Semiannually	1%
Annually	13%

Management has determined that each policyholder will receive a

Expense report

Name _____ Period ending _____

| Day | City and State | Lodging | Transportation | | Auto-mobile expenses itemize below | Meals — Itemize business meals below | | | Local taxi, carfare, tolls, etc. | Entertain-ment Itemize below | Misc. expenses Itemize below | Daily total |
			Air, rail, etc.	Limousine, car rental, etc.		Breakfast	Lunch	Dinner				
Sun												
Mon												
Tues												
Wed												
Thurs												
Fri												
Sat												
Totals												

Week's expenses

Number of days away from home _____
Number of days away from home on personal affairs _____
% of total days away from home spent on personal affairs _____

Nature or purpose of travel _____

Itemize all reimbursable expenses in appropriate blanks
Itemize on reverse side those expenses not reimbursed

☐ Deduct from my advance
☐ Mail to

Signature _____
Approved _____

Entertainment and business meals

Date	Name of person(s) entertained company—title	Time and place	Nature and purpose of entertainment	Amount	% or $ allocated to business

Automobile expenses

Date	Mileage-gas, parking, repairs, etc.	Amount

Miscellaneous expenses

Date	Items	Amount

Figure 5-7

118

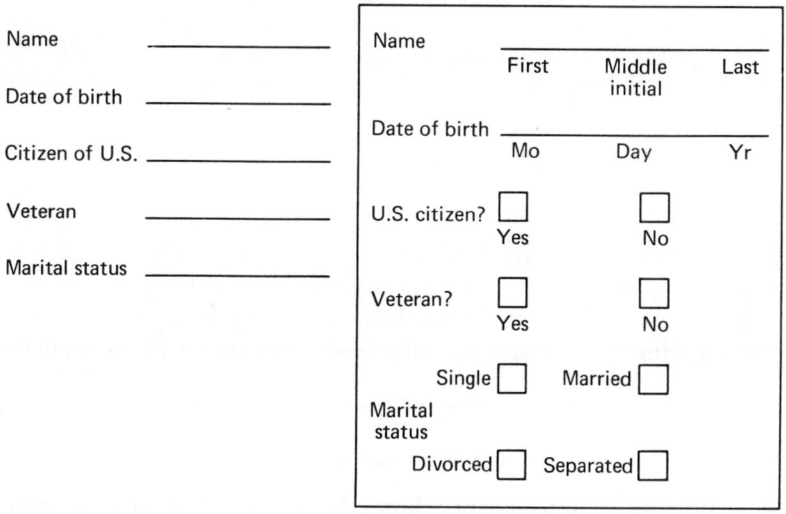

Fig. 5-8 Using check boxes in forms design.

notice for a premium due 2 weeks before the due date. It is anticipated that the policyholder will return the notice with a check for the proper amount and the returned notice will become an input document for the accounting system.

Recall that the computer configuration at Life Protection consists of a card reader, a card punch, four magnetic tape drives, two disk drives, and an IBM 1403N printer. Current plans call for the preparation of the premium notices on continuous-form paper. Use the turnaround document checklist to design the premium notice.

MINI-CASE 5.4

The Life Protection Society is currently redesigning its employment application form at the request of the personnel director. A routine review of the form's use reveals that it is the source document for establishing the basic personnel record of each employee. The personnel record has the following punched card format:

Employee Number	1– 5
Employee Name	6–20
Social Security Number	21–29
Date of Birth	30–35
Employment Date	36–41

Department Assigned	42–43
Sex	44
Starting Salary	45–51
Test Scores	52–61
Marital Status	62
Telephone Number	63–69

The application contains other information, such as home address, previous employment, education and training, and military experience. Life Protection uses about 600 of these forms each year.

Design an application form which will be appropriate for the personnel department's use and be suitable as a document for keypunching.

· GROUP CASE 5.1 ·

Maintaining the accuracy of the address file at the Life Protection Society is difficult. A survey conducted 2 months ago shows that 18 percent of the policyholders changed their address during the past year. Since accurate address maintenance is essential to the cashflow and public image of the company, Life Protection's management has emphasized that the procedure to ensure correct addresses be given top priority.

Change-of-address notices come in several ways: many are received on the back of the premium notice, others are received by telephone and are recorded internally, and still others come in letters. The original address is created from the application for insurance.

Not all changes are address changes. Some correct a mistake, or notify the office of a change in marital status. Sometimes, the policyholder is merely notifying the company of his correct zip code.

Your group has been designated to coordinate the forms design for address maintenance at Life Protection. You have been told to prepare the following:

1. The design of the basic address-change form.

2. The coordination of the address-change form with the premium notice.

3. The design of the portion of the Application for Insurance form from which the original name and address record is taken.

4. The design of the punched card that is used for the original entry in the address file.

5. The design of the punched card used for address changes.

The master address file has the following format:

Policy Number	1– 8
Name	9–23
Street Address	24–40
City	41–52
State	53–62
Zip Code	63–67

Consider these problems in your solution:

1. What can be done to develop an audit trail for tracing errors in the file?

2. Is there uniformity among the various forms in the system?

3. Consider the possibilities for error in the system. What are your forms doing to reduce these errors?

4. What steps can be taken to check the accuracy of the changes that have already been introduced into the system?

glossary

bursting   process of separating one form from another

coder   anyone who prepares input data for a computer system

coding sheet   document completed by a coder, designed to be a source document for keyed input

decolating   process of removing carbon paper from continuous-form paper

form   document with preprinted information and spaces for inserting data

NCR paper   chemically treated paper designed to produce multiple copies without carbons

photocopy   image or copy of an original document

source document   paper from which input data in a computer system are taken

stencil   special type of paper from which multiple copies can be made

turnaround document   form, usually produced by a computer printer, which becomes input data to a computer system

REVIEW QUESTIONS

1. What implications do key-to-tape devices have for designing input documents?

2. Explain some forms techniques that can reduce errors in a system.

3. List some forms with which you are familiar that have public-relations aspects for a business.

4. What factors should be considered when determining the size of a form?

5. What considerations must be weighed before adding another copy to a multiple-part form?

6. What should be considered when designing input forms?

7. Why should forms be designed for the convenience of the coder?

8. What should be considered in designing turnaround documents?

9. What factors are pertinent in designing output forms?

10. What purposes does forms design serve?

11. You have been asked to do a statistical analysis of the students in your class. What data do you wish to include in this survey? Design a form for gathering these data and a corresponding punched card for computer input.

12. Bring a sample of a turnaround document to class. Point out some good, and some bad, forms-design features in this form. For which input device was the form designed?

13. Give three examples where forms are used to create input for a computer system and serve other functions as well.

14. Bring to class an example of a multipart form. Does the form give adequate instructions to the person completing it? Can you determine how the form is processed internally wihin the organization that uses it?

15. A special report, produced on a printer, requires 50 copies. How would you go about producing these copies? Why did you select this method?

16. Give four examples of how check boxes can be used effectively in forms design.

part **III**

Developing
the System

chapter 6

The Feasibility Study

Objectives

You have now learned to use some of the elementary techniques of the systems analyst. You can flowchart, design forms, and set up a PERT network. You also know what a system is and how it interacts with hardware to achieve management's goals. You will now be able to use these techniques and concepts as you study how a company actually puts a computer system into effect.

Systems development has four general functions: planning, design, testing and conversion, and implementation. The effort that develops a plan for designing, testing, and implementing a system is called a feasibility study.

This chapter examines how a company selects appropriate areas for feasibility study, and how it conducts such a study. When the chapter has been completed, you should be able to write a clear and simple feasibility report with the aid of the checklists and examples provided.

SELECTING AREAS FOR SYSTEMS STUDIES

Corporate management has the responsibility of establishing a mechanism through which an organization can undertake systems studies in an
orderly manner. Generally, selecting appropriate systems for study is
done in one of several ways:

> 1. Management directs which systems studies should be undertaken.
>
> 2. The systems group selects the areas that it feels require investiga-
tion.
>
> 3. A selection committee is chosen with the authority to select areas
for study.

Regardless of the method used, selection of projects for systems
studies usually involves these steps:

> 1. Review and analysis of proposed systems changes
> 2. Analysis of the resources available to perform systems studies
> 3. Analysis of the organization's priorities

This review should result in one of three possible alternatives: the
proposed study is rejected and no further action is taken; the proposal
is accepted and the systems department is designated to initiate the
study; or the proposal is tabled until some time in the future (Fig. 6-1).

Proposals for changes in existing systems come from many sources.
Some, of course, are impractical and can easily be ruled out by who-
ever selects projects. Others are practical, but impossible to carry out
because of limited resources. Some perfectly good suggestions must be
rejected or tabled because more important proposals have priority.

The group making decisions on proposed systems changes is an
extension of corporate management. Top management must be instrumental in its formation and must authorize it to make binding decisions. It must be understood that when a proposal is approved by the
selection committee, corporate management is also approving it and
authorizing the feasibility study.

TYPES OF FEASIBILITY STUDIES

Proposed systems changes leading to feasibility studies usually fall into
one of three categories:

> 1. Changes to existing systems
> 2. Completely new systems
> 3. Hardware surveys

Most projects are undertaken to change existing systems. Some changes merely require a slight modification in the current system to accomplish management's goals. Other proposals can be so major that they influence the philosophy of the entire organization as, for example, the installation of a "total system." In a total system the entire organization is viewed as one large system, composed of subsystems, all functioning to achieve management's goals. Each individual and, in fact, every resource are viewed as systems components in achieving corporate objectives.

Most systems changes, however, start with an existing subsystem that has encountered problems, has proved inadequate, or has become obsolete.

Completely new systems are rare. They are usually instituted in new companies where precedent has not been established, or when an older company enters a new line of business. Occasionally, a new system will be created because the existing one is inadequate or so obsolete that it is valueless as a starting point for a better system.

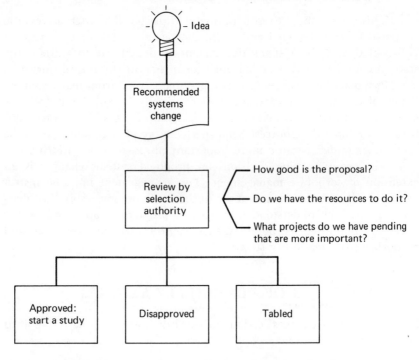

Fig. 6-1 The selecting authority can dispose of a suggestion in three possible ways.

Hardware surveys may be as simple as determining the best piece of peripheral equipment to be added to a computer system or as involved as deciding whether or not a computer is needed in an organization. Implied in a hardware study is the selection of a manufacturer or vendor. Since most computer equipment can do the job its manufacturer claims it can, the most serious consideration in selecting equipment is often determining which manufacturer best services and supports its equipment.

Another hardware decision that often results from a feasibility study is whether to rent or buy equipment. For many years computers could only be rented, and so it became traditional to rent. Now that they may be purchased, the overriding consideration is how long it will take the particular model to become obsolete. Data processing is a dynamic business and it has been normal for each new series of computers to make the preceding ones literally obsolete. As a rule of thumb, a corporation should rent unless it is quite sure that it cannot possibly go to new equipment within the next 4 years.

INITIATING A FEASIBILITY STUDY

The selection committee's job is to review proposals for change and authorize feasibility studies. All it really says, in effect, is: "This idea seems to have merit, so it would be worthwhile to have the systems people take a further look at it." This "further look" into a proposal is the systems survey or feasibility study.

The purpose of a feasibility study is to convert a goal desired by management into a plan to achieve that goal. The key step in starting a study is to appoint the person who will be responsible for the successful completion of the study, the project leader.

To successfully initiate a feasibility study, the project leader must accomplish two tasks: (1) he must clearly define the objectives of the study; and (2) he must devise an implementation plan so that the corporation can allocate the necessary resources to assist him.

A major problem in business is that systems analysts often spend much time solving the wrong problems. This is sometimes the fault of the selection committee, who might simply have used poor judgment in assigning priority to systems studies. Often, however, the mistake is made at the outset of the feasibility study because too little effort is made to clarify the objectives. Systems proposals should always be carefully documented, and every effort made to ensure that the group requesting the study and the project leader agree on the goals. No study should be initiated until management, the project leader, and the requestor of the study all agree on clearly defined goals and the ground rules to attain them. This agreement is accomplished by frequent and informal exchanges of ideas among the people concerned with the study. Documentation by memo is important, because memos formalize concepts that may be hazy unless written. But these concepts must be understood by all, and this is best accomplished through normal business conversations, meetings, and an occasional cup of coffee.

With the goals in mind, the project leader can devise a preliminary plan for conducting the study. This plan includes:

1. A statement of the objectives of the study.
2. An estimate of the scope of the study.
3. A list of the steps required to complete the study.
4. A rough schedule for the project.
5. An estimate of the human resources necessary to complete the study.
6. An estimate of the cost of the project.

CONDUCTING THE FEASIBILITY STUDY

After the objectives of the study have been agreed upon and a preliminary plan formulated, the actual study may begin. In general, feasibility studies go through these steps to achieve their objectives (Fig. 6-2):

1. Initial stage
   a. Defining objectives
   b. Forming a preliminary plan
2. Search stage
   a. Staffing the feasibility team
   b. Gathering and analyzing data
   c. Producing a preliminary plan
   d. Management review
3. Final stage
   a. Completing systems plan
   b. Formalizing proposal
   c. Producing a feasibility report

When the initial stage has been completed, the feasibility team may be chosen. In small studies, there may be no feasibility team, but rather an individual or even someone concentrating only part of his efforts on the study. More complex studies require groups with the collective expertise to devise a solution to the problem. Since a feasibility study usually requires knowledge from various areas in a business, there

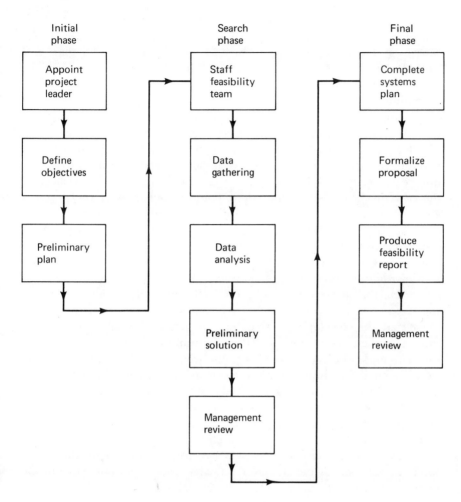

Fig. 6-2 Steps in a feasibility study.

is no reason for the feasibility team to be limited to systems people. Certainly the areas to be affected by the changes the feasibility study will recommend should participate actively in the study. Again, it is important that top management ensure that the talent necessary to do the study is available. So a typical feasibility team would consist of full-time systems analysts, specialists from user areas "on loan" for the duration of the study, and other specialists lending necessary expertise to the study on a part-time basis.

The first task of the feasibility team is to gather whatever data are needed to perform the study. But how many data are enough?

A feasibility study, properly conducted, should produce a carefully considered, complete plan that will satisfy the objectives of the study. Moreover, the feasibility group must be convinced that the plan will work and is the best solution available. The group must then convince top management and the user areas that their proposal is a workable, optimum solution.

Data gathering for a feasibility study consists of determining the causes for the current problem, how the problem is presently being handled, and what solutions are available. Analyzing the data starts with documenting the facts collected, usually in chart form, so that they can be understood. The basic document for analysis is a flowchart of the current system with annotations pointing out each of the problem areas. Data gathering and analysis will be treated in Chapter 7.

At this point in the feasibility study, a plan for the new system should begin to develop. As the plan develops, the feasibility team must consult top management and the managers of the user areas to avoid wasting time on unacceptable solutions. This preliminary review must determine that the evolving solution really meets the objectives set for the system. At this juncture, management should be appraised of the impact of the developing system on the financial and manpower resources of the organization as well as the impact on other systems. Management must also realize at this point what limits the realities of the working environment put on management's objectives. Plans that look good on paper may not work unless the proper work environment exists.

If corporate management, the user areas, and the feasibility team all agree that the preliminary solution is directed at the true objectives of the system, the study may be completed.

More data gathering, more analysis, further pursuit of alternative solutions, and much debate should finally lead to a cohesive solution to the problem. The solution will be explained in a formal feasibility report.

FEASIBILITY REPORT

The culmination of the feasibility study is the formal feasibility report. Ordinarily, the report is directed to corporate management, who must understand the implications of the proposal for the overall needs of the organization; user managers, who can evaluate the impact of the proposed changes on their areas; and the systems design team, who must put into practice the plan designed by the feasibility team.

Essentially, then, the feasibility report is a document for management's use, brief enough and nontechnical enough for a manager to comprehend its meaning and implications, yet detailed enough that the proposed system can be designed from it. A feasibility report could possibly be as short as one page or as long as 100.

The report may vary in content, depending on the application being studied, so there is no exact formula for writing one. However, normally it contains:

1. An outline of the proposed system.

2. A description of the input to and the output from the proposed system.

3. A definition of the files that will be created, made obsolete, or changed as a result of the proposal.

4. A definition of the potential trouble areas anticipated in developing the system.

5. A statement of the machine requirements for the new system.

6. An analysis of the benefits anticipated from the new system.

7. A cost estimate for the new system.

8. A plan for implementing the new system. This would include schedules for testing and converting to the new system.

9. A statement of the alternatives to the new system.

The ultimate design of the system must await management's approval. When a feasibility study has been conducted properly, disapproval of the feasibility report is rare because the report should contain no surprises. A feasibility team must develop and maintain good relations with all those connected with the study. Throughout the study it must involve management and the users in the developing solution so that the feasibility report is truly the work of many areas. The feasibility team develops the solution, and persuades those concerned to accept it, but it can accomplish this only when it has gained the confidence of management and the users.

Technically, the feasibility report is only a recommendation, but it is an authoritative one. Management has the ultimate authority to say "go" or "no go" or reopen the study because it is not convinced that the recommendation is best for the organization. Only with management's acceptance is the job of the feasibility team ended. Only then can the systems designers begin to wrestle with the realities of making proposed systems into existing ones.

The feasibility team should consider the following before recommending a solution to management.

1. Will the new system actually save money? If so, will the savings be

sufficient to justify designing the system?

    2. If the proposed system will cost more than the current one, can it be justified through one of the following?

        a. Management will receive better and more timely information on which it can make profit-making decisions.

        b. The customer will receive better service, leading to increased profits.

        c. The users will receive better service from the system, leading to increased production, more accurate data, or better morale. This is justifiable when it ultimately leads to increased profits.

    A proposed system must be justified to management on a cost versus benefits basis.

MINI-CASE 6.1

The payroll system at the Fenton Mole Sporting Goods Corporation is run manually despite the fact that the company has had automated equipment for 15 years. Four weeks ago, Ed Milosovich, the Controller, wrote a memo to Bob Mack, the Director of Data Processing.

TO: Robert J. Mack

FROM: Edgar Milosovich

DATE: May 15, 19--

RE: Computerizing the Payroll

    For several years we have discussed automating the payroll system but for one reason or another it wasn't feasible. I think the time has come to take another look at the problem.

    Within the past 5 years, we have expanded our staff from 375 to 1,200. The payroll section has only five people in it and because of the complexity of the payroll, with overtime, part-time, hourly and salaried employees, we find ourselves particularly hard-pressed to get the payroll out on time.

    A computerized payroll could accomplish the following:

    1. Payment of all employees on time.

    2. Over the long run, a substantial reduction in the cost of producing the payroll.

    3. As a by-product, we can generate statistics on employee utilization and turnover.

Would you give this suggestion high priority?

Three weeks later Bob Mack sent the following memo:

```
TO:   Edgar Milosovich
FROM: Robert J. Mack
DATE: June 6, 19--
RE:   Payroll Feasibility
     I met today with the feasibility selections commit-
tee and we have decided to do a formal feasibility study
of your proposal for an automated payroll system. We
think the timing of your proposal is good, and I have
assigned one of my finest systems analysts to conduct the
survey.


                    R. J. Mack
                    Chairman, Feasibility Committee
```

Bob Mack has appointed you project leader.

    1. Make a list of the questions you will ask Mr. Milosovich when you interview him.

    2. Make a preliminary plan for your feasibility study.

    3. What talent do you require on your feasibility team?

• GROUP PROBLEM 6.1 •

The student council at Harper Valley Junior College is concerned that there is no existing master file with student data available to it. The student council is considering compiling a roster of all students enrolled at the school. Harper Valley has a little over 7,000 students enrolled in various 2-year programs.

    Four weeks ago, Matt McGrath, the president of the student council, submitted the following memo to the Council:

```
As of October 1, there are over 7,000 students enrolled at
Harper Valley Junior College. As president of the student
council, I feel that it is essential that we have a record
of each student and a direct means of contacting each of
them. Moreover, since we have numerous requests from
students to produce a class roster, the compilation of a
master file on punched cards could provide us with the
basic information required. I recommend that the Council
appoint a committee to look into the possibility of pro-
ducing this file.
```

Your group has been appointed as a feasibility committee to look into President McGrath's request. A preliminary investigation determined:

1. The college administration has no punched card records that could be used to produce the master file.

2. The college will allow you the use of its computer at a minimal cost. The college has an IBM 360/40 computer capable of handling punched cards, magnetic tapes, and disk files.

3. The college will allow the student council access to the files it requires to complete its roster.

Conduct a meeting of the feasibility committee. What steps must your group take to complete its study? What questions do you have for Mr. McGrath? What data should the file include?

Prepare a report for the student council indicating the results of the meeting and the direction in which the committee will proceed.

• GROUP PROBLEM 6.2 •

TO: Dr. Charles H. Brane
FROM: R. L. Topping, Chairman, Feasibility Committee
DATE: May 15, 19—
Re: Proposed Student Registration System

The feasibility committee has concluded the following from its investigation into a proposed new system for registering students. It is clearly the objective of the administration to register all students with as little inconvenience as possible to the administration, the faculty, and the students. Moreover, the administration expects that any new system will provide the most service at the least cost to the college in the long run.

The committee considered three reasonable alternatives for attaining these goals:

1. Continuing with our current system of processing the student registrations at a local service bureau.

2. Developing a system using the college's administrative systems and programming staff.

3. Contracting with a consultant who is a specialist in this field to produce a system in conjunction with the college.

The committee recommends alternative 3.

Alternative 1, continuing with our current system, will never provide the service our college requires. The system, an all-purpose registration system, used in several hundred colleges, was originally adopted as a stopgap measure when student registration reached the point where manual processing was impossible. The current system eventually does get the students registered, but it has the following drawbacks:

1. The service bureau has conflicts in scheduling because other colleges have registration when we do. This results in errors in the schedules of 8 percent of the students being registered. Moreover, delays in processing have caused undue inconvenience on the part of both the faculty advisors and the students. Last semester, over 800 students and 35 faculty advisors waited for 3 hours for delivery of the student's schedules. All indications are that we can expect similar bottlenecks in the future.

2. For these past four years, the direct cost for student registration has averaged $18,000 per year. The committee feels that this outlay of money should result in a better service to the college.

3. The input to the registration system is used only once. The student's requests for courses is keypunched and he is given a schedule. These data should also be input to a master file of the student body available to the college on a permanent basis. The committee feels that it is ineffient to produce computer input data and use it only once.

4. The college has no control over the data after they have been completed in source form by the students. The service bureau keypunches and processes it along with the data from many other schools. The resulting inaccuracies are embarrassing and costly.

Thus the committee concluded that a system tailored to the needs of our institution would be advantageous. This system would be designed to give us the data base required to provide a college-wide management information system, as well as produce a student registration that would satisfy the particular needs of our institution.

To produce our "personalized student registration system," we considered two realistic possibilities: to produce it with our current staff, or to seek outside help.

The college administration currently employs one systems analyst and two programmers. Next year's budget requires that they spend their full time in developing a college payroll system and making necessary changes to the existing budgeting and reporting systems. Moreover, no one on the staff has had experience in student registration. To hire and train additional staff members would be more costly than contracting for outside help. The committee feels very strongly that using outside professionals will result in more meaningful data systems for the institution.

The committee submitted the following specifications to each of three management consulting groups.

"Harper Valley proposes to organize a system to register students and develop a data base for student records in conjunction with a management consulting firm. Harper Valley will provide the expertise to determine the precise data needs of the college. The college will also provide all clerical and keypunch services required by the new system. The college's computer will be available for programming and systems testing.

The management consultants will provide:

Detailed design of all input and output forms

Design of the master file

All computer programs necessary to satisfy the information requirements of the college.

The proposed system must be compatible with the college's current computer configuration."

Two of the firms have expressed a willingness to provide these services. Cost estimates were not submitted because the information needs of the college have not been defined. As a result of discussions with these consultants, the committee feels that both firms can provide the system required by the college. Both have a competent staff, experienced in this field. In fact, one firm only does this type of systems work. Both demonstrated that they had produced satisfactory work at other colleges.

The feasibility committee thus proposes that the college administration negotiate a contract with one of the two consulting firms as the best approach to providing the college with a satisfactory registration system.

1. If you were the college's president, how would you react to this report?

2. Compare the report with the checklist for feasibility reports. In what respects does the report satisfy the suggested contents of a feasibility report? In which areas does it fall short?

3. What other alternatives exist that the committee does not mention?

4. What additional information is required before systems design can begin?

5. What type of information should the college require from the consulting firm?

6. What type of information should the consultants seek from the college?

glossary

hardware survey   feasibility study to determine the equipment needs of an organization

project leader   person responsible for completing a systems undertaking

selection committee   corporate group charged with analyzing proposed systems changes and having the authority to initiate feasibility studies for those projects it evaluates as practical

systems survey   feasibility study

Review Questions

1. What is the role of management in a feasibility study?

2. What is the goal of a feasibility study?

3. What would you include in a preliminary plan for conducting a feasibility study?

4. Why are most computer systems currently rented?

5. What personnel would compose a feasibility team?

6. For whom is a feasibility report written?

7. What is included in a feasibility report?

8. Explain the three phases of a feasibility study.

9. What is the role of the project leader in a feasibility study?

10. What is meant by a hardware survey?

11. How do companies select appropriate areas for feasibility studies?

12. What type of data gathering is required for a feasibility study?

13. In your own words, what is a feasibility study?

14. Comment on this statement: "Systems analysts determine which systems are best for a company."

15. What criteria should a feasibility team consider before recommending a system to management?

16. What is meant by the phrase "cost versus benefits analysis"?

chapter 7

Data Gathering
and Interviewing

Objectives

To conduct a feasibility study, or for that matter, to carry out any stage of systems development, the systems analyst must know the facts. In this chapter you will learn where information is located in a company and how it can be uncovered.

Although a systems analyst must be an accomplished interviewer, interviewing skills are often taken for granted. You will learn how to conduct an interview, what questions to ask and how to ask them, and how to retain and organize the data collected.

You should also know the value of some other techniques in data gathering, such as work measurement, sampling, and questionnaires.

Data gathering takes place constantly throughout the systems development process. The selection committee gathers facts on which to base its decision whether or not to pursue suggestions further. The feasibility team gathers data in determining a workable solution to a business problem. The systems analyst needs data to design the system outlined in the feasibility study. Data associated with systems studies usually are obtained in answer to these questions:

1. What is the problem?
2. What is the company currently doing about it?
3. What tools are available to help solve the problem?
4. What other areas in the company are affected by the problem?
5. What opinions are available concerning solution of the problem?

Thus data gathering includes two general areas: facts and opinions.

SOURCES OF DATA

The first question the data gatherer must answer is: What is the problem? The answer to this should be developed in the documentation during the early stages of systems development. Each stage of the systems development cycle begins with a definition or redefinition of the problem. By the time the system is to be designed, the problem should certainly be defined. But this is not always the case. Sometimes the user staff, working with a system on a daily basis, has a much clearer concept of a problem than the people who participated in the selection committee or the feasibility study. Perhaps the apparent problem, a partially obsolete system, for example, is magnified by the real problem, poor morale among the user staff. Here, both the managers, who realize that the system is becoming obsolete, and the workers, who may be unhappy with corporate management, recognize a portion of the problem. The systems analyst must realize that a problem has more than one aspect and, like an iceberg, the obvious symptoms may be only a small part of the overall problem. To be effective, the systems analyst must realistically determine the various parts of the problem at hand.

To answer the next question, "What is currently being done about the problem?" the systems analyst must find out the current procedure. In a well-organized company, a complete set of procedures, perhaps illustrated with flowcharts, should be available. However, merely uncovering them and taking them at face value is a poor systems technique. Systems change, and very often the changes are not reflected in the formal documentation of an organization. Then, too, the procedure for an operation is not always followed.

In determining the current operation, the systems analyst must discover how the job is actually performed and must document these steps in written or chart form.

The tools available for problem solving are numerous. Hardware may have been developed recently that may solve the problem. But systems tools are not limited to hardware, they are often ideas; often people. Perhaps the company has hired employees who have the precise talent to handle a particular situation. Maybe the problem is organizational and hiring the right manager will improve things. The tool needed might be a system used successfully in another company and might be yours for the asking. The trade journals in the data processing industry are full of successful systems ideas that people are willing to share with you, sometimes free, sometimes for a fee.

The systems analyst must gather the facts surrounding a system. He must determine not only the precise steps making up a system, but also:

Volume of transactions
Peaks and valleys of occurrence of transactions
Cost of the various components of the system
Effect of one system upon others in the organization
Interaction between the organizational structure and system
Impact of the informal organization upon the system
Effect of company policy upon the system

Gathering opinions can be as important as gathering facts, but opinions are often colored by one's position in an organization. Generally, managers should have sound opinions on the overall implications of the system and the operating staff should be listened to in matters of systems details. Eventually, the systems analyst should be able to synthesize these opinions, and provide a workable, even optimum, solution to the problem.

Other sources of data are available to a systems analyst; for example:

1. Company's formal records
   a. Accounting and statistical reports
   b. Organization charts
   c. Existing data processing charts
   d. Minutes of various committee meetings
2. Existing systems documentation
   a. Written procedures
   b. Flowcharts
   c. Programming documentation
   d. Various departmental files
   e. Files maintained by individuals
3. Written sources outside the organization
   a. Government publications
   b. Material published by computer manufacturers

    c. Publications of professional organizations, corporations, or systems professionals

4. Opinions and data from other sources
    a. Friends and associates in the systems field
    b. Data disseminated at seminars and conventions
    c. Informal conversation with businessmen

PROCESS OF DATA GATHERING

Data are gathered by five basic methods:

1. Interviews
2. Observation
3. Sampling
4. Meetings
5. Research

Interviews

A systems analyst spends much of his working day interviewing people. Some analysts are very successful in an interview and come away knowing considerably more than before the interview. Other systems analysts find that an interview adds little or no information to that already uncovered by their research. The difference may be attributed to the interviewing ability of each.

Systems interviews are classified into two types: "knowledge worker" interviews and management interviews. In conducting the interviews in a systems study, the systems analyst usually starts with top management and works his way down through the various levels of management to the actual workers in the system. This is reasonable because the managers should supply the analyst with the generalities concerning the system, and the operating staff should fill in the details.

management interviews

In a management interview, the systems analyst must determine:

the overall picture—What is the importance of the current systems study? How does it relate to other systems in the organization?

the goals of the system—What does management really expect the system to accomplish?

the ground rules—What resources will be available to the systems department? What possible alternatives should be ruled out?

To conduct the interview well, the systems analyst must prepare thoroughly. Specific questions should be formulated. At times, it is appropriate for the systems analyst to prepare a brief agenda to be certain he will cover every pertinent area during the interview. Managers usually consider their time precious, and do not look favorably upon nonproductive interviews. Know the subject well before interviewing a manager! Chances are he knows the area well and there is no better basis for a fruitful conversation than when the two people involved are knowledgeable in the subject matter.

A systems study requires management support because it is from this support that the systems analyst derives his authority. The systems analyst must receive a clear dictate from management to initiate a study so that he can interview, use, or consult with the people in the organization who must participate in the study.

A management interview is generally carried out in a more formal atmosphere than an interview with a knowledge worker. It is usually conducted in the office of the manager, which often puts the systems analyst at a disadvantage. As in sports, the home grounds have a distinct advantage.

Management interviews are not necessarily conducted between only two people. Whenever possible, it is an asset to have someone with you when you interview. Very simply, it gives one person time to think while the other asks or answers questions.

Many management interviews are conducted in a formal manner, but the mood must not become too formal, for then there is no free exchange of ideas and the result is often misunderstanding or a generally nonproductive interview.

knowledge worker interviews

Systems analysts are not always welcomed among the staff of an organization. Many workers feel threatened by the computer, often for legitimate reasons. Other workers, particularly factory employees, confuse the systems analyst with the time-and-motion expert. A systems analyst must remember that the goals he is supposed to have in mind, the objectives of the corporation, are not necessarily foremost in the minds of the people he is interviewing. So he cannot safely assume that every worker in the company is eager to bare his soul to the systems analyst and let him know all the details of his job. The realities of business are not that simple.

To interview a knowledge worker, the systems analyst must provide the proper atmosphere in which to conduct an interview, and some of that responsibility must be shared by corporate management.

Ideally, when a new system is being developed, or a computer being introduced into a company, corporate management issues a statement that no one will be terminated as a result of the impending changes. This ordinarily is not too much for management to concede. If the changes will really cut back the number of jobs at a company, normal attrition will usually account for more-than-enough departures. What usually happens is that the jobs of many people are modified, not eliminated, by the changes in a computer system. For a systems analyst to do his job properly, corporate management should specify that it will make every effort to retain the people affected by the new system. A systems analyst cannot be expected to get full cooperation from someone who feels the system being developed will replace him.

The systems analyst must be a reasonable, likable person in an interview. The person being interviewed must feel that he can trust the systems analyst and respect him as a fellow knowledge worker. Only on these bases can a reasonable exchange of ideas begin.

Knowledge workers must be treated with respect. They know something the systems analyst does not know, and this is the basis for the entire interview. Systems analysts often speak in terms of "picking someone's mind," but this attitude leads to resentment on the part of the interviewee and results in a less than complete exchange of ideas.

In business, the most fruitful conversations come about in an informal atmosphere; people discuss business problems more readily over a cup of coffee. The need of the knowledge worker to feel comfortable in an interview must be satisfied. The interview will only be as good as the atmosphere in which it will be conducted.

The key to a successful interview is the interviewer's preparation. Much wasted conversation can be avoided if the interviewer familiarizes himself with the job of the person he is interviewing. One obvious sign of preparedness is a list of questions or a checklist of items to be covered in the interview. In some instances it may be appropriate to send the person to be interviewed a list of the items you wish to discuss so that he will also come prepared for the interview.

It usually is acceptable to take notes during the interview to be certain that the interviewer retains a sufficient amount of the discussion. Moreover, it is a good idea to summarize an interview in writing and send the summary to the person interviewed. In effect, the interviewer is asking; "This is what I think you said, please check to see whether or not I understand you correctly."

Tape recording an interview often arouses suspicion and inhibits a knowledge worker from speaking freely.

Ordinarily, an interview with a knowledge worker goes deeply into detail. The interviewer must be a skilled questioner and an alert listener to comprehend all the details he may be told during an interview. Thus, in most effective interviews the interviewer does very little talking. A technique to get an interviewee to "open up" is the use of the open-ended question. This means that questions are asked in such a way that they cannot be answered by a simple "yes" or "no." Contrast these two questions: "Do you like your job?" and "What are the things you like about your job?"

The second question should provide more information for the interviewer. In an interview, a person can only learn when he is listening and not talking.

Observation

The most reliable data a systems analyst may obtain are gathered through observation. They are free of most of the biases that may color data acquired through other sources. Ideally, data gathered by observation are used to verify the accuracy of other data.

Information received through interviews requires verification. People may not deliberately lie, but very often they misrepresent facts or reply to questions for which they really do not know the answers. One has a tendency to act like an expert when being interviewed, and experts do not like to be asked questions they cannot answer.

Gathering data through observation may be done several ways. A systems analyst should gather a sampling of *completed* forms from the existing system. Blank forms may deceive a systems analyst because they indicate only the way the forms designer anticipated the data would be received. A cross section of completed forms will indicate much better how the forms are actually being used.

It is often helpful for a systems analyst to spend some time in the user area either watching the operation of the current system or actually participating in it himself. This serves two purposes: (1) the systems analyst gets to know the users and perhaps will be better able to satisfy their needs; and (2) the systems analyst obtains a more realistic view of the actual data in the system.

Just by being in the area where the current system is being performed, the systems analyst learns a great deal that he would never discover through an interview or a cold review of the statistical data associated with the system.

Work Measurement

The systems analyst must know the volume of transactions and the time and cost to complete specific tasks. Many organizations have established administrative work measurement programs to provide corporate management with data to evaluate performance, establish budgets and controls, analyze costs, and improve scheduling. These programs can be a prime source of data for the systems analyst.

When a work measurement system does not exist, a systems analyst may, with the cooperation of the supervisor in the user area, set one up on a temporary basis. The objective of such a program is to determine precisely the volume of data moving through a user area and precisely how long it takes to process these data. The systems analyst can also determine the bottlenecks in the existing systems and should become more aware of the exceptions to normal processing and how they are handled.

Work measurement programs, when handled poorly, produce problems. People are sensitive about having their productivity measured, especially in a white-collar environment, where it is not often done. Such a program should only be instituted when the data anticipated from the program are vital to the systems study.

Sampling

A critical decision for the systems analyst is how much data is enough. To review every transaction in a given system for a year is obviously too costly and may confuse more than clarify. Analyzing three or four transactions from a system that processes thousands in a year may be economical, but will probably lead to disaster. The analyst must evaluate the cost in data gathering against the benefits he will derive from the data.

The two basic methods of sampling are random and systematic. In a random sample there is no plan for selection and thus no biases, because each item in a group has an equal opportunity to be selected. Statisticians provide the basic techniques for gathering random samples. An example of systematic sampling is transmittal to a systems analyst of a copy of every hundredth transaction from every tenth desk. Both methods are widely used in systems studies, but the systems analyst must determine the size of the sampling in terms of the knowledge that he expects to gain from it.

Questionnaires

Questionnaires are efficient when the systems analyst seeks a small amount of data from a large group of people. The questionnaire must be worded carefully so that the meaning of each question is clear to most of the readers. In some instances questionnaires may be coded so that the results can be keypunched and the data compiled by a computer.

Questionnaires lack the personal touch so vital for a free exchange of ideas. The person completing the questionnaire cannot have questions clarified, and he will tend to be brief in his answers and not volunteer as much information as he would in a normal interview.

Meetings

A well-conducted meeting is a fine source for gathering data. Bringing together the users and the systems designers allows each to hear what is on the mind of the other. A meeting can often clarify the relationship of one department's work to another's in a proposed system. In fact, meetings are often a revelation to the users. Frequently overheard at such a meeting are statements such as: "Oh, is that what happens to that report after we complete it . . . I always wondered what use you people had for it."

Research

Some systems problems are solved only through careful and tedious digging through various documents. Trade magazines, professional papers, textbooks, and government documents provide tremendous volumes of material in the rapidly changing field of data processing.

Data Analysis

Data analysis naturally follows data gathering. In most systems studies, more data are gathered than can be conveniently handled. The systems analyst must learn to summarize data and display it graphically to facilitate analysis.

The systems department should provide facilities where legitimate data analysis can take place—a conference room, located near the systems department, is often appropriate. Here the systems analyst can meet with users and other systems analysts to examine the displays of the gathered data. Here, perhaps, the systems analyst may obtain the answers that he requires to produce an optimum solution.

Systems displays, such as flowcharts, merely tell a systems analyst what is being done in a system. One of the purposes of systems analysis is to determine why certain functions are being performed. Knowing why procedural steps are performed should lead to improved ways of doing them and the elimination of unnecessary steps.

The key word in analyzing data is "Why." Why is this form currently produced in five parts? Why must the master file be copied onto a second disk pack every day? Why can't the input data be checked more closely at the terminals?

The systems analyst must avoid quick solutions to problems. He should design systems that will be fairly permanent, and this can only be done with painstaking, thoughtful, time-consuming analysis. This implies scheduling sufficient time for data analysis throughout the entire systems development process, but especially in the period immediately preceding systems design.

MINI-CASE 7.1

In the cases for this chapter, one student will portray a systems analyst interviewing an employee of LaFemina Fashions and a second student is to act as the employee.

LaFemina Fashions has been in the woman's retail clothing business for 43 years, and the post–World War II boom created tremendous growth within the organization. Since 1945 the number of employees has grown from 46 to over 400. Unit record equipment was installed in 1957 to do accounts receivable. In 1963 a second-generation computer replaced the unit record equipment, and inventory and payroll systems were added to the machine accounting applications. It took 5 years to iron out many of the problems created by the new equipment and systems, and just as the dust was settling, the corporation installed a third-generation computer. All the data processing work of LaFemina Fashions is currently being done on this third-generation equipment, but the systems are generally the ones developed back in 1963.

The Case of Walter J. Proper, Chief Accountant

Walter J. Proper started with LaFemina Fashions as an assistant bookkeeper over 35 years ago. Walter is a very good bookkeeper and has given the company 35 years of dedicated service. In 1958 he was promoted to chief accountant, a position he still holds. No one knows more about the details of the accounting at LaFemina Fashions than Walt Proper, and no one has been more critical of the computer's problems than Walter has. Walter is usually a pretty friendly guy; he is always polite, but there is something about systems analysts telling him how to do his job that really irritates him.

Just last week, the executive vice-president had too much money deducted from his paycheck. "Why can't that computer of yours calculate my pay correctly?" he thundered at Bob Walsh, the manager of the systems department. Bob has asked you to look into the problem.

A preliminary check on your part indicates that the executive vice-president had submitted the proper form for adding one dependent more than a week before the payroll was distributed, but somehow Walt Proper's people in the payroll department did not get the transaction into the system on time. When you reported back to Bob Walsh, he instructed you to go see Walt Proper to straighten the matter out. On your way up to interview him, all you can think of is the last time you talked to Walt about payroll. "Yessir," he kept saying, "back in the old days when we did payroll by hand we didn't have all the mistakes you have today."

MINI-CASE 7.2

The Case of Willie Warren, Data Center Supervisor

Willie Warren is the supervisor of the data center at LaFemina Fashions. Twelve years ago he came to LaFemina Fashions as a machine operator and in 3 years he was appointed tabulating supervisor. In the old days, he wired the tab boards, ran the jobs through the machines, and literally was king of the installation. As the business grew larger, the machine room grew, but Willie became comparatively less important in the overall corporate picture. Now there are programmers and systems analysts, many of whom make more money than he does, who do not have his knowledge about the details of the operation. It got to the point where last month he applied for a programmer's job within the organization, but he was turned down because he only received a "C" on the aptitude test. "You're very valuable to the organization where you are" they told him, but he didn't really buy it.

Willie has had a constant complaint concerning the systems department. For years, he maintains, the systems department has never turned over adequate documentation for the systems they installed. Last week, Willie wrote a memo to Bob Walsh detailing some of his complaints. His memo said in part:

Last Thursday, one of your programmers changed the daily inventory program without telling anyone. Unfortunately, now it requires a date card when previously it didn't. My night operator wasn't aware of the change, and was unable to do the run. In fact, it took me over an hour the next day to figure out the problem because your programmer was on vacation. Can't we tighten up the controls over our documentation?

Bob Walsh has turned the problem over to you. You first checked with the programmers and you kept getting the same type of answer. "Who has time to worry about his stupid instructions?" "They pay me to write programs and they always want them out the day before yesterday." "Even when I give them good instructions, they foul up the job anyway."

It is time to interview Willie to see what can be done to improve the situation.

MINI-CASE 7.3

The Case of Ms. Steele, Professional Buyer

You are a member of a team designing a new inventory system for LaFemina Fashions. LaFemina currently produces a quarterly listing of its entire inventory. The inventory file is on magnetic tape with changes to file recorded on punched cards. Your team is developing a master inventory file on disk which will be updated and displayed daily. Management feels that if the people in the organization have timely information on what is currently on hand, better decisions will result in profitability for the company. The purchasing department's performance is expected to improve considerably as a result of the new system.

The buyers have been considerably unhappy with the current system. "We keep buying things we have in stock, and we have no idea of what we need" is the chronic complaint of the buyers.

You have been asked to interview Ms. Steele, the assistant buying manager. Ms. Steele has been a buyer for over 25 years, 15 of which have been with LaFemina. Ms. Steele has a reputation as a cool, shrewd businesswoman who distinctly does not like "computer people." "Technicians," she calls them. "They really don't understand the business needs of professional buyers."

You must find out from Ms. Steele what information she requires from the new system. She is, no doubt, the most influential buyer, and you are certain that she will be the most critical of anything that goes wrong in the new system.

You feel that you are being fed to the lions, but her opinions are clearly needed. Interview Ms. Steele.

---

glossary

informal organization normal relationship of people in a business environment, independent of organizational charts

knowledge worker any person who earns his living by what he knows about a particular job

procedure series of related steps making up a portion of a system

sampling selecting a group of transactions or events from a whole

work measurement system for evaluating an individual or a group's productivity through work counts and timing activities

REVIEW QUESTIONS

1. Write five open-ended questions for an interview with a knowledge worker.

2. List some formal records available for data gathering in most companies.

3. Give instances of data gathering in the systems development cycle.

4. Besides the actual steps making up the procedure, what else must a systems analyst determine when investigating the current procedure?

5. What are the basic methods for gathering data?

6. How does a systems analyst go about determining the current system for a given application?

7. Besides computer hardware, what are some of the systems tools used for data processing problem solving?

8. How does a systems analyst prepare for interviewing a knowledge worker?

9. Where do management interviews differ from interviews with knowledge workers?

10. What is the importance of opinion gathering in data collection?

11. It is said that defining the problem is the essence of systems analysis. How are problems defined? Who is responsible for defining them?

12. List four types of formal records, available in most companies, from which an analyst may extract systems data.

13. How may a systems analyst extract data through observation?

14. Comment on this statement: "Computers eliminate jobs in an organization."

15. Why is it advisable to use completed forms and not blank forms when gathering data?

chapter **8**

Systems and Data Base Design

Objectives

The feasibility study provides a plan for designing, testing, and implementing a system. But much work must be done before the plan of the feasibility study becomes the system in operation.

In this chapter you will learn to design a system in detail. This includes organizing the system so that it can be designed, designing the master file, or data base, and designing the input and output records. Moreover, the design effort must be controlled so that the data in the new system will be current and correct.

153

SYSTEMS DESIGN EFFORT

The systems design phase of the systems development cycle takes the proposed system from the feasibility study through detailed program design. It progresses through various stages, beginning with the generalities of the feasibility study and ending, hopefully, when every detail in every program fits neatly into place.

Feasibility studies are not always as detailed as this text suggests. Often, the systems designer gets little more than ""We'll do it this way" or "We'll get this hardware device" to work with. It is not unusual, especially in small companies, for the systems designer to formulate his own general as well as detailed plans.

The systems designer usually starts with a review of the hardware and software available. This includes investigating software packages available to facilitate conversion or implementation of the new system. Next he will think through the solution proposed by the feasibility team to search for pitfalls that might be apparent to him but not to the members of the feasibility team. He next must add more detail to the design schedule as he should be more aware now of the problems the proposal presents and of the resources available for the project.

Systems design progresses through several stages, becoming more detailed in each stage. The feasibility study is the first step toward systems design, a plan to attain corporate objectives. The systems designer must convert this plan into a smoothly operating system.

The general tasks in systems design are:

1. Designing the overall process
2. Segmenting the system into workable modules
3. Organizing the data base
4. Specifying the programs to achieve the systems objectives
5. Designing the input and output documents
6. Designing controls for the system
7. Documenting the systems design
8. Designing the master file
9. Systems review

Data gathering and analysis continue throughout the entire process of systems design. The primary sources of data for systems design are:

Present procedures
Similar systems in other organizations
User personnel
Corporate statistics
Manufacturer representatives

DESIGNING THE OVERALL PROCESS

Systems design starts with determining the requirements that will fulfill the objectives of the system. The systems designer must decide the steps to be taken in the new system, who will take these steps, and how they will be accomplished. At this early stage, the design team produces a general flowchart that demonstrates the scope of the system. From it the remaining tasks may be organized.

SEGMENTING THE SYSTEM
INTO WORKABLE MODULES

A system of any reasonable size is divided into logical components, or modules, for organizational purposes. A module consists of a series of related operations that have similar design considerations. Modules are segmented into computer runs. What can be accomplished by each computer run is determined by the core capacity of the computer, the input/output devices available, and natural groupings of related tasks.

ORGANIZING THE DATA BASE

A data base is a collection of all the information related to a specific application and may be composed of manual, card, tape, and disk records, or any combination of these. It must be organized so that information may be added to it and data extracted from it as easily as possible. Some terminology associated with data is:

> *data element*—one item of information, such as a field or a code
>
> *record*—group of related elements
>
> *file*—group of related records
>
> *data base*—all the information related to a specific application
>
> *data bank*—integrated system of files providing information on a variety

of applications

SPECIFYING THE PROGRAMS
TO ACHIEVE THE SYSTEMS OBJECTIVES

The feasibility study defined the goals that the system is expected to attain. The systems design team produced a general plan to achieve these objectives plus a design of the data files that will be included in the system. But specific objectives are accomplished through computer programs.

The first step in program design is to outline the objectives of each program. Here, the systems analyst acts as a problem definer and the programmer acts as a problem solver. The analyst must determine which programs interact with others and how they interact before the programs can be written.

DESIGNING INPUT/OUTPUT DOCUMENTS

Programming cannot begin before input and output specification are clearly defined. Normally, samples of input and output forms are provided for the programmer as documentation. Before doing this, the systems analyst will check each form with the user personnel. There must be an opportunity to try out input documents under realistic circumstances, and users must see proposed output so that they may have an opportunity to tell the analyst whether or not they find the forms suitable and efficient.

DESIGNING CONTROLS FOR THE SYSTEM

Systems controls ensure proper functioning of the system in three areas:

1. Correct processing of data by the system being designed
2. Correct conversion of the data from the current system to the new system
3. Accuracy of new data being created for the system

The accuracy and completeness of data in a new system are essential and cannot be taken for granted. Totals must be established for the number of records, dollars, and any essential item of data in a system, and these totals must be compared regularly with corresponding totals of the data as they exist at various points in the systems development. The systems designer must be certain that his data remain complete and unchanged. Moreover, control totals must be conveniently subtotaled to expedite correction when errors occur.

Other controls are established in the way of checkpoints in the systems design process at which progress may be measured and evaluated.

DOCUMENTING THE SYSTEM

Complete documentation, including flowcharts, decision tables, written procedures, and detailed forms design, must be prepared during the systems design phase to explain the systems plan to the data processing professionals and user personnel. Often, documentation is neglected until the system is fully designed and conversion is imminent. This leads to hastily prepared documentation and does not allow user personnel adequate time to familiarize themselves with the new system.

In all computer systems, adequate documentation must be prepared for the programming group:

> General flowchart of the system
> Listing of all the runs in the system
> Finalized version of all input/output forms
> Layout of all files affected by the program
> Detailed explanation of the coding structures to be used
> List of known exceptions to the system

DESIGNING THE MASTER FILE

A typical data processing system includes a master file of records that is regularly changed through transactions. To design a system, the analyst must determine the basic structure of the master record. First he must identify the controlling field, that field that distinguishes one record from another. It usually contains a number, such as the customer number, item number, or social security number. After the controlling field is identified, the systems analyst identifies each element that will be required in the record. Sometimes the normal requirements of the system make many of these elements obvious. For example, a billing file must always have the customer number and amount owed. Beyond those obvious elements, data elements required vary according to the needs of the particular system.

Two sources for identifying data element requirements are the elements in the current system and the elements proposed in the systems specification. The systems analyst must determine what he needs to achieve the objectives of the proposed system. He must also analyze which proposed data elements are extraneous or whose cost to gather and maintain would exceed the benefits to be derived.

After an entire basic master record is composed, a storage medium must be selected. Several factors affect this decision:

> Storage media available (you do not order disk packs when you currently have none and the application being converted is a small one)
> Length of the record—(a record of 100 characters cannot fit on a punched card)
> Volume of file activity

Retrieval requirements of the system
Size of the file

Master files are dynamic in that they are subject to change through input transactions. Thus a design consideration is the interaction between the master file and its input transactions. Moreover, a file is a source of information. The frequency of inquiries into the file and the method of displaying the status of the file are important factors in the choice of the storage medium.

The systems designers must determine the most convenient sequence for the file. Will it be alphabetical or numerical? What will be the controlling field? Must the file be maintained in sequence?

Master files constantly interact with the transactions that affect them. The systems designer must coordinate this interaction by carefully designing the transaction format. Initially, the systems designer determines how the transactions are currently processed. Specifically, he must know:

Types of transactions currently in use
Their current format
Their current volume
Anticipated changes in the type of transactions
Effect of the transactions on the growth or shrinkage of the file

Then the systems analyst must incorporate the changes required by the new system and develop complete and concise transaction formats.

Data files must also interact with hardware. In batched processing, tape files must have their records grouped into convenient blocks to facilitate input/output operations. Determining record and block lengths are an integral part of systems design.

The master file must be designed to facilitate output, to provide easy retrieval of data through a minimum of programming.

THE SYSTEMS REVIEW

When the master file, hardware configuration, and transaction formats are designed, and the details of the work flow largely worked out, the project leader should conduct a systems review with the key user personnel. This may be the last chance to avoid possible breakdowns in the developing system. The systems review should be a step-by-step account of the proposed system as it is now planned. Active participation, criticism, and approval by the users is essential so that they will feel that the evolving system is to a large extent theirs and is not being imposed by systems outsiders.

The systems analyst is concerned with compiling every aspect of data. He must, therefore define each data element, and combine elements into logical records, the records into files, and the files into a workable data base. Implied in organizing these data is the choice of the storage medium. The essential consideration is whether or not the data must be accessed directly. If so, a direct access device, such as a disk, will be needed. Data that can be displayed adequately through printed reports may be stored on magnetic tapes or punched cards.

PROBLEMS IN FILE DESIGN

The systems analyst must complete the design of the entire master file before programming begins, since programmers require the master file layout as part of normal documentation. It is not enough merely to compile all the necessary data elements and combine them in a master record. The file designer must be concerned with how much data he can extract from existing files and what he must create. The cost of creating data in machine-readable form is enormous, especially when there is a large volume involved. In practice, much discussion and manipulation goes into creating the elements of a file. When users suggest that a particular item be included in a master file, they must be made aware of the cost of producing the item in machine-readable form originally, and how much it costs to maintain it for the duration of the system. Systems designers must insist that the users think through how they will use each item in the data base. "Oh, we'll find a use for it someday" is not sufficient. The users must demonstrate the necessity of the data and how its use will justify the cost of gathering and maintaining it.

Systems design requires careful thought for each field in a record. Will a name field have the first or last name first? Ordinarily, the first name will be first, except when a file will be maintained in alphabetical order. Will hyphens be put in number fields? Not when their location is consistent, as in a social security number. Hyphens may be edited into a field through a computer program. How many positions must be reserved for a name field?

MINI-CASE 8.1

The Last Chance Dating Service has been having too many mismatches lately. Ms. Dolly Levi, the vice-president, has asked you to design a new master file for prospective dates. "We simply do not have the right data in the files to match people up," she said last week. "Can you imagine arranging a date for a guy who looks like Tom Jones with a girl who looks like Phyllis Diller?"

What data do you think belong in Last Chance's master file? Document your ideas with a card or tape layout.

MINI-CASE 8.2

Swankee Fashion Shoppes is automating its payroll for the first time. Swankee has 1,100 employees, all of whom are salaried and paid biweekly. There is no overtime payroll in the organization. There are no deductions from salary except those required by law. All Swankee's employees have state and federal taxes withheld.

You have been asked to do some of the preliminary systems design work on the proposed payroll system. Specifically, you must define the data elements that are common to all payroll systems. Document these elements in the form of a tape record layout.

MINI-CASE 8.3

FRIOCALOR manufactures appliances for the home. Its line includes refrigerators, stoves, dishwashers, washing machines, dryers, and refuse compactors.

FRIOCALOR requires its customers to send in a form to activate the guarantee for each appliance that it sells. From these forms it intends to develop its direct mailing file. FRIOCALOR currently sells over 100,000 appliances per year.

The marketing department of FRIOCALOR feels that people who are satisfied with a FRIOCALOR product are quite likely to buy another one. They are also interested in analyzing the patterns in which appliances people buy. For example, what is the possibility of someone who has bought a washing machine buying a dryer within the next 18 months? In which geographic areas do specific products sell? Where do the higher-priced models sell? Which retail outlets sell which products?

Design a data base for the master address file. Construct coding structures for the data they will require. Design the guarantee form for the customers to complete.

• GROUP PROBLEM 8.1 •

Harper Valley Junior College has had an IBM 360/40 for three years. The computer has been used exclusively for educational purposes as all the college's data processing work has been done either manually or at a service bureau. Dr. Charles H. Brane, the new president of Harper Valley, has put the creation of a management information system near the top of his priorities for the next two years.

The college's administrative systems department, in conjunction with a faculty committee and the representatives of the student council, conducted a feasibility study for developing a management information system. The group concluded that first priority should be given to computerizing the student's records. The feasibility report anticipated that the master file for the system would be contained on a disk pack. The system would be designed to produce:

1. A report card after each semester, which will be mailed to the student's home. The report would include the grades for the semester completed, all previous grades recorded at the school, the grade average for the current semester, and the accumulated average.

2. A transcript, upon request.

3. Statistical data for the registrar's office.

Students graduating from Harper Valley usually accumulate 64 credits, but a few have completed over a hundred credits at the school. All courses are worth either 3 or 4 credits. The system requires that credits completed at other colleges and transferred to Harper Valley be indicated. Harper Valley uses a letter grading system (A, B, C, D, F, W).

1. Determine what statistical data should be contained in the master file.

2. Design the master record.

glossary

data bank   integrated system of files providing information on a variety of subjects

data base   all the information related to a specific subject area

data element   smallest unit of a data processing record; roughly the equivalent of a field on a punched card

file   group of related records

module   component of a system or a program

record   group of related fields

software package   program or collection of programs that may be rented or purchased

Review Questions

1. What are some of the tasks in the systems design phase? Explain the role of the systems analyst in each.

2. What are some of the different types of controls required in systems development?

3. What documentation must be prepared for the programmer during systems design?

4. What factors determine the basic storage medium for a specific system?

5. Which factors determine what a computer run can accomplish?

6. What is meant by systems control?

7. What is a software package? Under what circumstances can they be used effectively?

8. What is a module? How is this term used in systems design?

9. What is a data base?

10. Which sources are used for collecting data for systems design?

11. Explain the hierarchy of data in terms of elements, files, records, data bases, and data banks.

12. Showing proposed output to users is an essential of good forms design. Why is this step so important?

13. How is the accuracy and completeness of the data in a new system verified?

14. What is a controlling field in a data processing system?

15. What is meant by the statement: "Master files are dynamic."?

16. What must a systems developer know about the processing of the transactions in a current system before he can determine how they are to be processed in the proposed system?

chapter 9

Systems Testing
and Conversion

Objectives

When the system has been designed, every aspect of it must be tested before the new system goes into effect. The processes of testing and conversion are closely related and must be coordinated by the systems analyst.

   This chapter will explain the different techniques used in testing and converting computer systems. You will learn the steps in testing a system and how to coordinate programming with systems testing. It is important to learn what constitutes a valid test, how much testing is enough, and how to determine when the system is ready to be converted.

   An existing system may be converted to a new one by means of several different strategies. For example, it is sometimes advisable to continue the old system for a period of time concurrently with the new one. At other times it is best to stop the old system as the new one is started. You will learn the factors to consider in decision making on conversion strategies.

   After you have completed this chapter you will be expected to develop a plan for conversion to a new system.

New systems, like new inventions, must be thoroughly tested before being accepted. Testing a new system on every level is particularly important with today's sophisticated and complex computers. Conversion to new systems is a way of life in data processing as new equipment, advanced techniques, and the corporate needs force constant changes in existing systems, yet very little thought has been given by systems people to effective testing and conversion techniques. Systems conversion includes four general areas: planning a conversion, testing all levels of a system, converting to the new system, and analyzing the new system in operation.

TESTING A SYSTEM

Systems do not work automatically; in fact, they usually are effective only after a long process of trial and error. Systems testing has three distinct phases: program testing, string testing, and systems testing (Fig. 9-1).

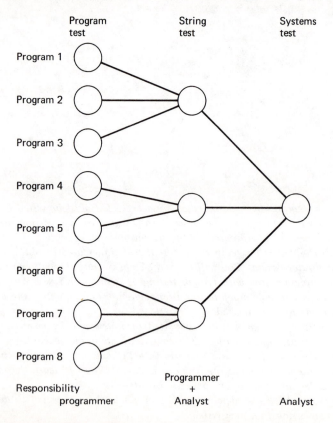

Fig. 9-1 Steps in testing a system.

PROGRAM TESTING

A program, to be running satisfactorily, must compile correctly, handle test data accurately, and tie in with other related programs.

Compiling a program correctly is largely a matter of proper grammatical use of a programming language. Achieving an error-free compile is clearly the responsibility of the programmer.

Programs may be tested with two types of data: live data and test data.

A programmer must test each condition in his program with test data. If, for example, a program calls for executing data with codes 1, 2, or 3, the program must be tested to see how it handles each of these codes, as well as any code greater than 3 or less than 1. The programmer must eliminate the likelihood that surprises occur during the life cycle of the program. Often data that are considered "impossible" at the time of programming mysteriously appear soon after the program is operable.

Each condition in the program must be tested. This implies a rather extensive test file for trying out each condition. Creating this file is largely the responsibility of the programmer.

Test data are designed with predictable results. Sample input is prepared and the anticipated results calculated manually. These results are then compared with computer output to verify data validity.

Test data check normal transactions and possible errors. Some data are created with deliberate errors in it to see whether or not the proper error messages are printed by the computer. Other transactions should contain multiple errors to see whether the programmer has anticipated these possibilities.

A program may be further tested with live data, that is, data that will actually be used in the proposed system. Usually, the systems analyst supplies these data often by taking transactions being processed by the current system and transforming them to the input forms of the developing system.

Complex programs require both types of data. Testing with live data demonstrates that the program is designed to anticipate future contingencies. This type of test may be used to demonstrate that the program can handle the volume of transactions it must when the system is operable.

Besides testing the program's ability to handle errors, the program test should verify that the program's counter capacity is sufficient for the volume of data it will process and that the program can perform the various mathematical functions required of it.

Large programs are the product of several programmers, each with a specific section, or module, to complete. Each module in these programs must mesh with the other program modules. Thus a part of programming testing is the coordination of the components of individual programs.

STRING TESTING

Virtually every program interacts with other programs. The output from one may be the input to another. As each program is completed and successfully passes the logical tests prepared for it, it is then tested to see that it fits in with related programs in the system. The systems analyst responsible for each portion of the system must test his entire module with both test and live data before the entire system is tested.

SYSTEMS TESTING

The testing process culminates in the systems test. In systems testing, the entire system is put through a dry run until it is considered operable. Operations and user personnel should participate actively in this phase to make conditions as realistic as possible.

Systems testing requires careful preparation. First, the project leader, the systems analysts, programmers, and users must agree on the test objectives. They must determine specifically what the systems test is expected to demonstrate and what constitutes satisfactory performance.

Test cases, processed through the system from start to finish, are used for systems testing. All concerned should participate in selecting test cases. The project leader and his staff must also provide a test procedure so that the operations staff can run each step without systems department help. Finally, the project leader must work out a test schedule that will provide time to perform and evaluate each step. The schedule must also take into consideration the normal activity peaks and valleys of the user and operations departments.

Systems must be designed to be tested. Milestones must exist in each system through which results may be compared with previously established standards. Thus systems testing must be as thoroughly planned as any other phase of systems development.

The systems test should be as realistic as possible. The operations and user personnel should carry out each step as directed by the procedures developed for the new system. When error messages are produced, the error-correction procedure should be carried out to ascertain its effectiveness. Moreover, the systems test should test the overall data flow in the new system, particularly to determine how well the computer system interacts with the clerical procedures associated with the system and how well the system interacts with other systems in the organization.

A system may occasionally be overtested, but that is rare. Testing is insurance against future problems—when the insurance is too costly in proportion to the risk, less insurance should be taken. The extent of testing is determined by several considerations:

> Complexity of the system
> Importance of the system to the survival of the company
> Life expectancy of the system
> Financial and personnel resources available

Systems Acceptance

User management is responsible for determining whether the system is performing satisfactorily or not. Systems must satisfy users. A system that may be considered perfect by a systems analyst is really unsatisfactory if it is not acceptable to the users.

Before testing begins, users and systems personnel must agree on acceptable standards of performance and establish parameters for accuracy for data in the system.

The people responsible for each aspect of systems testing are:

> *users*—validity of data
> *project leader*—interaction of systems components
> *systems analysts and programmers*—program accuracy

Gaining formal and realistic acceptance of a system by the users is important because they are in the best position to determine whether the system is acceptable, especially when they have been involved from the beginning in the systems development process. The systems department does not have the right to impose unacceptable systems upon users.

SCOPE OF A CONVERSION

The term "conversion" is freely tossed about in data processing circles with a variety of meanings: "We're converting to a 370." "The inventory conversion is ready to go." "Did you convert that program to COBOL yet?" There are three different types of conversion: a hardware conversion, a systems conversion, and a program conversion. Although the term "conversion" usually connotes a radical change from an old method to a new one, it also is used to describe small changes to existing systems. Each type of conversion has a different impact on a business organization.

The systems group may find it difficult to define the scope of a conversion. The problem resolves itself only with an extensive and free exchange of ideas among users, systems analysts, and data center personnel. Even the simplest type of conversion, the routine change to an existing system, requires careful examination and testing before implementation. Some conversions affect the entire organization. Obviously, many conversions fall somewhere between the extremes of a routine change and a corporate-wide conversion, and thus require extensive data gathering before their impact can be anticipated. The systems group must determine the effect the impending changes will have on all facets of the organization:

> Existence of the corporation
> User areas immediately concerned with the change
> User areas remotely, but realistically, concerned with the change
> Systems and programming departments
> Computer center
> Profits and/or customer service

In evaluating the effects of a conversion, two primary factors must be determined: (1) the impact of the changes, and (2) the drain of the corporate resources.

PRELIMINARY CONVERSION PLAN

The feasibility report normally contains a preliminary plan for testing and converting to a new system. This plan should include the following:

> Test schedule
> Description of the major files that must be converted
> Conversion schedule
> Some indication of the magnitude of the conversion and how much manpower it would require
> Basic ground rules of the conversion, such as who will determine when the conversion is ready to be implemented

A conversion plan is evolutionary. Systems design will alter many of the goals anticipated by the feasibility team. The importance of producing a plan during the feasibility study is threefold:

> A plan in existence gives everyone concerned some feel for the general area in which they are operating.
> Deadlines and checkpoints may be established.
> Distinctions may be drawn between target dates and "can't miss" dates

Selecting the Method of Conversion

The feasibility report should recommend a method of conversion. This recommendation should be a synthesis of opinion among the feasibility team, user management, corporate management, and the systems group. The decision is an important one and can have serious effects upon the resources of an organization.

The three standard methods of conversion are *immediate conversion, parallel conversion,* and *pilot conversion.* Most frequently used, however, is a gradual conversion, a combination of two or even three of the methods.

immediate conversion

The immediate, or "stop-and-go," conversion is the simplest, cheapest, and most risky. In it the old system stops at a given date and the new one begins. Implied in this method is the assumption that the new system has been thoroughly tested and will not fail. In an uncomplicated system where the results do not vitally affect the operation of the corporation, this can be a highly efficient conversion method. Sometimes conditions dictate the use of an immediate conversion. For example, the old system may be totally incapable of handling the current volume of transactions, or the new data base and the old one are completely dissimilar, or, perhaps, new equipment is not compatible with the old equipment.

parallel conversion

Implied in a parallel conversion is that the old system continues until the new one is working satisfactorily. Traditionally, the old system was continued for one normal cycle (in accounting applications this would be 1 month) and if the new system was working properly, the old one would be discontinued. Today's systems are more complex than previous ones, so a parallel conversion requires careful planning. When a parallel conversion method is adopted, the definition of a "working system" and the performance standards for the new one must be formulated. A parallel system drains the resources of an organization tremendously. If the parallel state lasts for an extended period, it conceivably doubles the cost for producing the same result, as the system is literally being done twice. Yet it is still not as costly as going into an immediate conversion and losing all continuity of the system with a resultant loss of revenue or customer service.

pilot conversion

In a pilot conversion the new system is constructed, tested, and operated in a controlled environment before it is installed. With this method an entire system can be tested by the people who will monitor it when it is in operation. Moreover, when the same system is to be installed at various locations, a pilot system can be worked out at one location and transported to the others. A pilot conversion is an excellent training device because the new system can be thoroughly debugged before installation. It is costly since the construction of an entire system in a simulated environment and the commitment of user personnel to test it puts a serious strain on the resources of an organization. In a company that is already pressed for computer time, finding time to construct and test a pilot system is difficult.

gradual conversion

The gradual conversion combines at least two of the other methods. In a large systems conversion, often a portion of the proposed system is relatively simple and can be installed immediately. This is ideal, particularly when there are immediate benefits to be gained through implementation of the change. The rest of the system may be installed in modules as each component is ready for operation. Each module must be fully tested, particularly in its relationship to the modules that preceded it into operation. This type of conversion requires careful project control to ensure that a vital part of the operation is not lost for a period of time.

The selection of a conversion method ideally should be determined during the feasibility study by the users and data processing management. In large-scale systems changes, corporate management should be a party to the decision because that decision can greatly affect the economic life of the corporation. Thus the feasibility report is the ideal vehicle for proposing and gaining acceptance of a conversion strategy.

Conversion Plan

The preliminary plan of conversion must be flexible. Remember, the feasibility report is merely the presentation of a plan to solve a corporate or a systems need and that the preliminary conversion plan is only a small part of the suggested solution. The feasibility report is offered after a reasonable amount of data gathering, particularly in the management areas. But the detailed design of a system uncovers new problems and greater complexities, and, as a result of intensive data gathering, the conversion schedule usually must change. The conversion plan is developed to coordinate the efforts of people from many areas of the company as well as to pull together the various aspects of the new system.

The following are some factors to consider when formulating a conversion plan:

Interaction of the program test schedule with existing operations

Interaction of the systems test with existing systems

Availability of key people to convert to the new system

Machine time available for conversion

Peaks and valleys in the normal work flow of the areas concerned with the conversion

Morale of the people who will perform the conversion

Complexity of the files to be converted

Relationship to other projects being conducted during the conversion

Delivery date of equipment that will be used in the new system

Availability of needed software

Status of training in the data processing and user areas

Controls needed to ensure a complete and accurate conversion

Preparation time for new forms

Priority of the new system in the minds of corporate management and the user areas

Timing in converting the various modules of the new system

A conversion plan is far more complicated than marking some dates on a calendar. The project leader is responsible for coordinating all the segments so that they will fit together in a logical, orderly fashion. A conversion plan can be summed up in two phrases: getting the people ready and getting the data ready.

All the factors to be considered in a conversion are not always known at the outset. The first schedule is merely a "best guess" which will be followed by other best guesses as more information becomes available. However, at some point the conversion plan must be confirmed, and all efforts directed toward meeting the critical dates on time. The time for confirming the schedule is determined by the project leader, who is in the best position to evaluate the status of the components of the system.

Conversion Schedule

Conversion schedules, often displayed as PERT charts, should highlight the critical steps to be accomplished, other contingent steps, and the control points through which realistic progress can be measured. Control points are used for comparing actual with projected progress and verifying the accuracy of the data being converted. The project leader must determine at the outset which control points are crucial and what alternatives are available when unexpected results occur.

The conversion schedule increases in accuracy as conversion time approaches. The schedule results from the interaction of the systems designers with the systems users and is subject to management approval. Smooth systems conversions occur only when planned properly. Systems analysts must realize that a new system is often introduced into an environment in which the people are fully occupied with the existing system, and therefore the conversion cannot be scheduled as if it were the only event taking place.

MINI-CASE 9.1

The General Kernel Food Company is a small producer of breakfast cereals and baby foods. General Kernel's line of 14 products is distributed nationally but is most popular in the north-central states. The company has its general offices in Detroit, with three plants located in other cities in the Midwest.

General Kernel has used computers for over 12 years and currently has two IBM 360/30s installed. Its computer systems have always been quite adequate, but management is studying the feasibility of modernizing the data processing within the organization. Currently, five basic master files exist for each of the following applications:

> Distribution analysis
> Customer billing
> General accounting
> Production control
> Inventory control
> Payroll

Each master file is on magnetic tape, and although summary information from one file is sometimes used as input for another, the master files generally operate independently of one another.

The feasibility team, of which you are a member, is about to recommend a consolidation of the data processing effort. They will recommend acquiring a larger and faster IBM/370 Model 135 and using only one computer instead of two. The feasibility team is working on developing one integrated data base for every application except payroll. Their philosophy is: "We should be able to get a total picture of each of our products. How much did it cost to make it? Who is buying it? What are the trends in its sales? How does it contribute to corporate profitability? How does its performance compare with our other products? How does our product get to the ultimate consumer, and at what cost?"

There is no doubt that the committee will recommend organizing a direct access computer system.

The company realizes the difficulties that it will encounter in developing the new system, but all indications are that management will give a green light to the project.

The feasibility team has turned up the following projections for the proposed system:

1. It will take 18 months to plan and create the new data base. Twenty percent of the data must be created from sources not already on magnetic tape.

2. The conversion will provide the opportunity to clear the files of incorrect and extraneous data.

3. The company anticipates cost savings from the elimination of redundancies among the files and cheaper computer rental.

4. Management will be able to obtain the data it requires for making adequate decisions on such matters as continuation of product line, proposed new products, and effects of marketing campaigns.

5. The current systems and programming staff will have to be supplemented with people experienced in direct access methods.

6. The proposed hardware configuration can be delivered within 13 months.

7. Every job in the current system can be emulated on the new hardware.

8. Programs for the new system will take about 14 months to write.

From the data given, do you think that General Kernel should convert to the new system?

You have been asked to write a preliminary conversion plan as a part of the feasibility report. You realize that this plan will change as other facts become known, but it will be the starting point in the conversion planning process. Include a strategy for conversion in your recommendations.

MINI-CASE 9.2

General Kernel has decided to convert to the IBM 370 system. Develop a preliminary testing strategy. Include in your plan:

1. The levels at which the system should be tested
2. The job titles of people who will be responsible for testing
3. The probable sources of test data

4. A rough test schedule

5. Some ideas on how to prove the validity of the test data

Document your plan in less than two typewritten pages.

———————◆———————

glossary

control point   milestone in a conversion at which time the status of events is evaluated

gradual conversion   combination of the more basic types of conversion in which the old system is converted piecemeal to the new

parallel conversion   strategy in which the old system continues for a time while the new one is being installed

parameter   a reasonable limit for valid data

pilot conversion   conversion strategy in which a workable model of the proposed system is constructed and tested until it is working properly

serial conversion   conversion strategy in which the old system stops the day the new system begins

string test   stage in systems testing where programs in the same systems module are tested to see how well they interact

REVIEW QUESTIONS

1. Briefly explain the process of testing a data processing system.

2. Describe the two types of test data. When is each type appropriate?

3. How does one determine how much testing is enough?

4. Explain each of the basic methods of conversion.

5. Explain the impact of a conversion on the various areas of an organization.

6. What is meant by the expression "A conversion plan is evolutionary."?

7. What must a project leader consider in setting up a systems test?

8. What are some of the considerations in the formulation of a conversion plan?

9. What are the four general areas of systems conversion?

10. What is a systems test? Who participates in it?

11. Who determines whether a system is performing satisfactorily?

12. What is a hardware conversion?

13. Which two factors must be considered in evaluating the effects of a conversion?

14. What is normally included in a preliminary plan of conversion?

15. Even if we know that a conversion plan will change, why is it advisable to always have one?

16. Under what conditions may an immediate conversion be advantageous?

17. What dangers are risked in a parallel conversion?

18. Under what conditions are pilot conversions appropriate?

chapter 10

Documentation in
Data Processing

Objectives

You are now familiar with each of the principal areas in systems development; planning, design, and testing and conversion. Each of these areas requires specific documentation.

In general, documentation becomes more detailed as the system develops. Planning documentation may be in outline form; documentation for systems design is very detailed.

In this chapter you will learn to produce appropriate documentation for various systems requirements, including documentation for programming, computer operations, and user and management needs.

Documentation has four purposes in data processing:

> Communication
>
> Instruction
>
> Specification of performance criteria
>
> Creation of historical data for future reference

There are five major types of documentation:

> *program documentation*—block diagrams, flowcharts, decision tables
>
> *operations documentation*—operator instructions, the run book
>
> *user documentation*—procedures, manuals, illustrations, charts
>
> *management documentation*—summary manuals, memos, statistical and

planning charts

> *systems documentation*—memos, reports (including feasibility reports)

systems design specifications, plans, file descriptions, input/output specifications, control points

PROGRAM DOCUMENTATION

All companies talk about programming documentation, but most do very little to see that it is provided. Before a program is begun, the systems analyst should provide the programmer with the required documentation. The logic in some programs is best described by a block diagram; decision tables are most appropriate for others. Programmers should insist on adequate documentation before starting a job.

Four items constitute minimum documentation required for each program (Fig. 10-1):

> Copy of all input/output documents affecting the program in final form
>
> Statement of standards for coding structures and input/output layouts
>
> Clarification of the program's interface with other related programs
>
> General block diagram or decision table

The programmer's responsibility in documentation is to provide information to enable another programmer in the future to make whatever changes are necessary. Personnel turnover is a normal part of business, and turnover is particularly high among programmers. A company can never assume that a programmer assigned to a specific program will be available in two years when changes are required to that program. For continuity of information, a company must insist on complete and meaningful documentation. Typically, a documentation folder is provided for each program, and it contains all the input/output forms asso-

Program specification

Input

Input data is taken from 3 cards (see layout format)

Code 1	Statistical card
Code 2	Address card
Code 3	Grade card

Sequence is code (80) within Social Security number (1-9)

Calculations

Quality points = grade X credits

A = 4
B = 3
C = 2
D = 1
F = 0

$$\text{Index} = \frac{\text{Total quality points}}{\text{Total credits}}$$

Output

Printed output, detail listing course number, grade, number of credits, and quality points. Printout to include the calculated index and the student's mailing address. Provide appropriate column headings.

Fig. 10-1 Minimum documentation required to write a relatively easy program.

ciated with the program, a detailed block diagram or decision table for the program, and a set of operator and user instructions (Fig. 10-2).

Maintaining this type of documentation is costly and time consuming and programmers do not like to spend their time doing this type of work. Routine changes occur frequently in a program and all changes must be recorded in the documentation folder. But these very changes which require updating existing documentation are the reasons for maintaining accurate documentation. It is difficult enough to follow the logic of another programmer's work without the added complication of having the existing documentation differ from the actual program.

One way of easing the programmer's documentation burden is to rent or buy one of the available software packages for block diagramming programs on the computer. These programs are expensive, but they free the programmer for programming instead of documenting.

In all forms of documentation, a critical factor is whether or not the benefits derived from the documentation justify the expenses involved. The programming manager must determine how much documentation is required at present to offset costly wasted time, errors, and delays in the future.

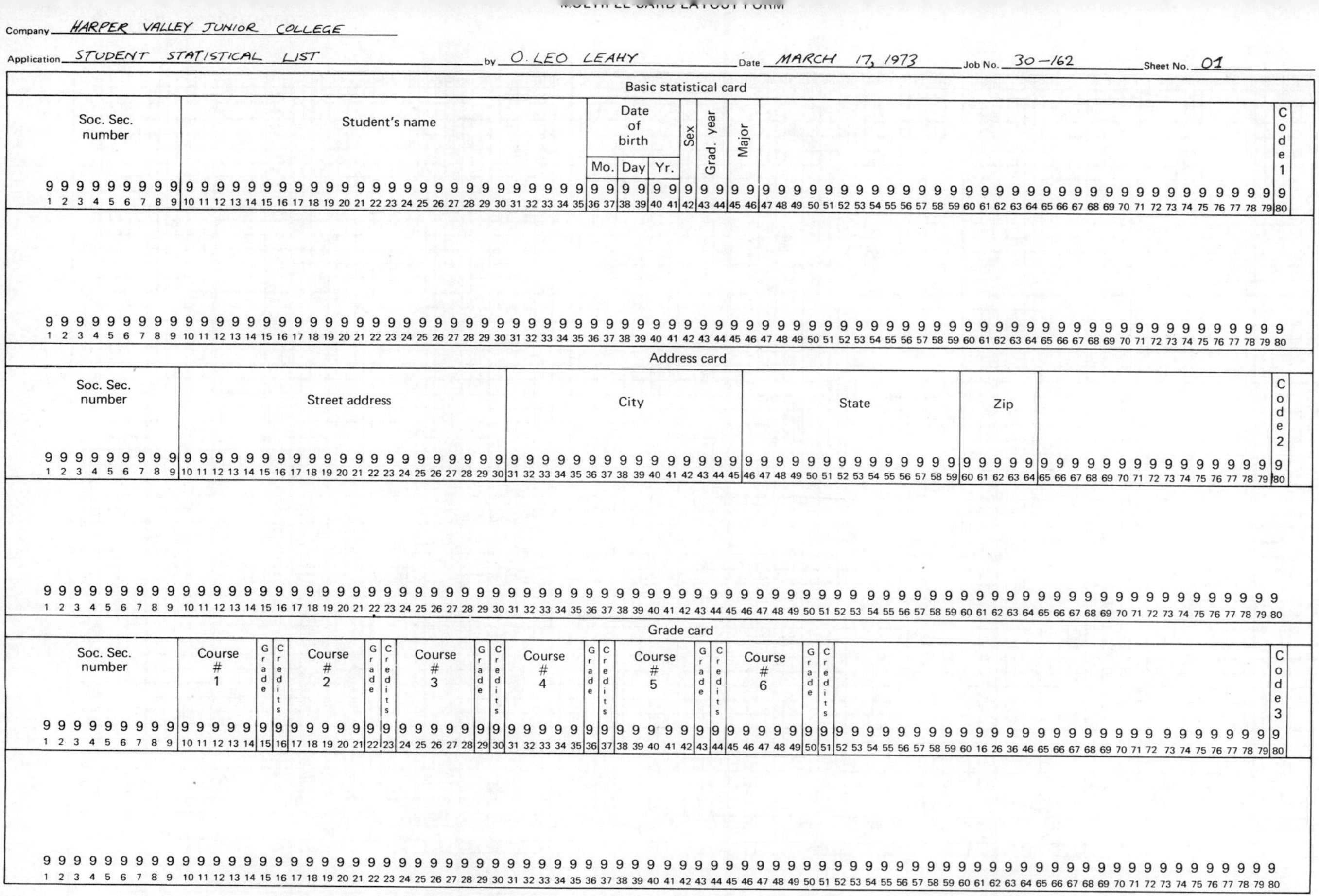

Company __HARPER VALLEY JUNIOR COLLEGE__

Application __STUDENT STATISTICAL LIST__ by __O LEO LEARY__ Date __MARCH 17, 1973__ Job No. __30-162__ Sheet No. __01__

Basic statistical card

Code 1

Soc. Sec. number

Student's name

Date of birth — Mo. Day Yr.

Sex

Grad. year

Major

Address card

Code 2

Soc. Sec. number

Street address

City

State

Zip

Grade card

Code 3

Soc. Sec. number

Course #1 Credits
Course #2 Credits
Course #3 Credits
Course #4 Credits
Course #5 Credits
Course #6 Credits

Figure 10-2

179

Fig. 10-2 Continued.

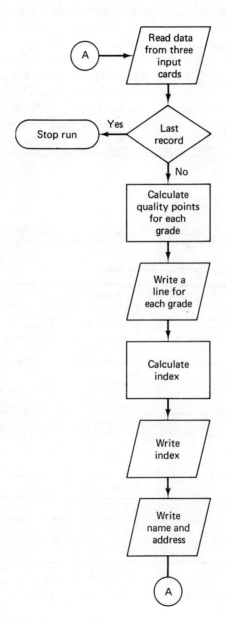

Fig. 10-2 Concluded.

OPERATIONS DOCUMENTATION

A well-designed system may run for several years with little or no assistance from the systems department. This can happen only when the system has been adequately documented (Fig. 10-3).

For a system to run smoothly, the computer console operator must understand the details of his job well. Providing the computer center with a set of operating instructions is not enough. The instructions must be in a form that is readily accessible to the operator and written in a style he can understand. A systems analyst must discuss in detail all the

Program name	Program number	Programmer
PAYROLL UPDATE	P-41	RAY MILLER
System	Frequency	Requestor
PAYROLL	WEEKLY	ROUTINE RUN

Run description

WEEKLY   PAYROLL   UPDATING   PROGRAM

Input/output instructions						
Device	Unit	Use	File description	Source	Disposition	Comments
TAPE	180	I	PAYROLL MASTER (1 VOL)	LIBRARY	LIBRARY - 60 DAYS	SIGHT CHECK DATE
TAPE	181	I	WEEKLY TRANSACTIONS	CONTROL	LIBRARY - 60 DAYS	
TAPE	182	O	NEW PAYROLL MASTER	SCRATCH	LIBRARY	
PRINTER	OOE	O				

Printer instructions			
Form	Tape	Vertical spacing	Comments
3 PART STANDARD	# 3 STANDARD	6 LINES/INCH	SEND TO PAYROLL SECTION

Special operator instructions

Figure 10-3

requirements of new jobs with the operations personnel before he can consider the job properly turned over.

The run book is traditional in computer centers. It is a collection of operator instructions for each program at an installation and typically contains:

1. narrative describing the run
2. listing of the programmed error conditions
3. detailed information for running the job, including:
   a. input/output forms to be used
   b. anticipated problem areas and how to handle them
   c. detailed description of the file assignment of each input/output device
   d. disposition of the data files after job completion
   e. general block diagram of the programming logic
   f. restart procedures

The run book usually takes the form of a loose leaf notebook because of the ease of substituting sheets when programs change. And now the development of the disk file and the CRT present another form for operations documentation: some installations write their operator instruc-

Message log		
Message #	Message	Operator action
P ∅ 1	WRONG MASTER FILE	CHECK DATE ON INPUT MASTER FILE. IT SHOULD BE 1 WEEK PRIOR TO TODAY'S DATE
P ∅ 2	INVALID TRANSACTION CODE	RECORD DISPLAYED. NO ACTION TAKEN.
Job control information		

```
//   JOB  P-41  PAYROLL  UPDATE
//   OPTION  DUMP
//   EXEC · P-41
/*
```

Fig. 10-3 Continued.

tions on a disk and display them on a CRT when required by the operator.

USER DOCUMENTATION

Systems users require adequate documentation both to prepare for a developing system and to smoothly carry out existing ones. To meet this requirement, each system should have a manual that contains everything the users must know to do their job properly. Users require two general types of information: complete detail to handle each case the system processes, and an overall picture of the system so that they can see their role in the total operation of the company.

The manual should supply the following specific information:

General flowchart of the system
Assignment of responsibility for specific tasks
Standards for work flow, including target dates and deadlines for specific tasks
Sample input and output documents
Detailed procedures
Anticipated exceptions and instructions how to handle them
Accuracy standards for data in the system

The systems department must write a thoroughly detailed narrative of each system, including the proper handling of routine cases, as well as exception handling. A staff member in the user department must have an authority to consult with when faced with a case that he has not handled before. He can turn to a supervisor, but a supervisor is not always available, or he can consult the systems analyst when problems occur, but this makes the systems analyst an advisor to the user areas and takes him from his proper role as the architect of new systems. A well-written manual can provide the information needed by the user, and it is always available to him.

Supervisory personnel in user areas must understand the overall picture in each system, just as staff members must understand the details of their function. This requires documentation in the form of charts, graphs, and illustrations so that the supervisory personnel have a clear grasp of their department's role in the total system.

MANAGEMENT DOCUMENTATION

The documentation required by corporate management differs greatly from that needed by users. The systems designer must be aware of management's needs and provide documentation to enable management to perform three functions:

1. Evaluate progress on systems development
2. Monitor existing systems
3. Understand the objectives and methods of new and existing systems

Management's primary need is to know in general the system's overall objectives and basic operations. A brief manual highlighting the key steps in each system may be prepared for management's use. Good managers have an exceptional ability to get to the heart of a system, and their experience should enable them to extract information from a systems summary or chart which may not be apparent to the systems analyst.

SYSTEMS DOCUMENTATION

Each phase in the systems development cycle is accompanied by appropriate documentation. The systems request, even if it is initially made verbally, eventually must be written. It is desirable for the user making the request and a systems analyst to work jointly in writing the request, since each can contribute knowledge the other does not have. The written systems request is merely a statement of the user's problem.

In documenting the results of its deliberations, the selection committee must specify the following:

1. The objectives of the impending feasibility study
2. The extent of the authority of the feasibility team
3. The individual or group responsible for completing the study

The feasibility report is probably the most important form of documentation in the systems development cycle. It accomplishes two purposes:

1. It states the objectives of the proposed systems change in reasonable detail after a sufficiently detailed study.
2. It presents a plan to attain these objectives.

The documentation of this plan must be thorough enough to enable the systems designers to produce a complete and effective system, and it should include a general flowchart of the proposal, generalized input and output specifications, and a general data base design.

At various points during systems design, the design team produces additional forms of documentation:

file specifications—detailed definitions of each file in the system, best done in graphic form *transaction specifications*—detailed descriptions of each type of input in the system, including a layout of each transaction and a narrative description of how it is used

output specifications—detailed descriptions of all output anticipated from the system, including an explanation for each item in every output

test plan

conversion plan

training plan

During the life cycle of the completed system, the system itself must provide documentation on how well it is operating and it should thus be designed to yield data about itself as a normal by-product. When transactions are taking too long to process or errors are too common, the system should automatically accumulate and display these data so that appropriate action may be taken.

PROJECT DOCUMENTATION

Controlling a systems project requires another set of documentation. The project leader must establish a reporting mechanism to alert him to developing problems and to enable him to inform management of project status. The basic format of project documentation is a list of checkpoints or milestones. This may be done with a PERT chart and must yield data in three areas:

time—Is the project behind or ahead of schedule?

cost—Is the project over or under budget?

quality—Does the project produce the desired outputs?

MINI-CASE 10.1

Chatham Electronics maintains a separate payroll for its hourly employees. There is an hourly rate for each employee and all employees are eligible for time-and-a-half pay for all time worked in excess of 40 hours per week. The employee's social security number and hours worked during the week are keypunched onto a weekly transaction card. The remaining data for each employee are contained on a magnetic tape master file.

Chatham pays its hourly employees weekly with a check written on the computer. Year-to-date information is updated weekly and stored on an output master tape. The only deductions from the gross pay are federal and state income tax.

Design the master record and transaction format.

Document the program specifications for a programmer to follow in writing the updating–checkwriting program.

---

glossary

interface   interaction of one phase of a system with other phases

run book   collection of operator instructions for running each program

Review Questions

1. What are the purposes of documentation?

2. Give some examples of systems documentation.

3. What is the minimum amount of documentation a programmer should expect before beginning a program?

4. How does a company determine how much documentation is enough?

5. Explain the function of the run book.

6. How much documentation should users expect?

7. What are management's documentation needs?

8. Define the documentation responsibilities of a programmer.

9. What purposes does a users' manual serve in a system?

10. Describe how a system in operation can provide documentation to evaluate its effectiveness.

11. What is project documentation? In which areas must project documentation provide data?

part IV

Systems of the Seventies

chapter 11

Direct Access and Teleprocessing Methods

Objectives

In this chapter you will begin applying what you have learned to current data processing applications.

The primary use of data processing systems today is with direct access equipment. The unique feature of direct access equipment, that it can process data when they are not in sequential order, materially affects the way systems are organized and carried out. You will learn to organize direct access files so that they will process data faster and retrieve information more quickly. Moreover, you will have a better understanding of the impact of teleprocessing equipment upon today's data processing requirements.

DIRECT ACCESS SYSTEM

The typical computer system of the 1970s has resulted from three hardware developments in the 1960s:

Direct access devices large enough and economical enough for the medium-sized computer user

Telecommunication devices to transmit large quantities of data

Various terminal devices that can transmit and receive data

The computer manufacturers can now produce the hardware necessary to handle most systems needs, but user organizations often lack the technical and managerial expertise to use this hardware to its full potential. This difficulty is evident in three primary problem areas: compiling and organizing a data base, programming a direct access system, and organizing an inquiry network.

Current systems fall into three major categories of processing:

batching—all the transactions for a particular period are saved and enter the computer system as a group, or batch, of input. Punched card and magnetic tape systems are all batch-processed.

on-line—the various input and output devices have access to the master files through the computer. An inventory system, where purchases and sales are recorded remotely and transmitted to update the master inventory file directly, is an example of an on-line system.

real time—a form of on-line processing where the response from the computer to the area from which an inquiry is sent is so prompt that decisions at these remote areas are based upon and controlled by the computer's response. Some classic real-time applications are the airlines reservations systems, Project Mercury, and the New York Stock Exchange reporting system.

DIRECT ACCESS HARDWARE

The three basic types of direct access hardware are magnetic drum, magnetic disk, and magnetic film strips. All three have the ability to find a particular record without reading through the entire file, but each has its own way of doing it. The drum rotates under a group of read/write heads until they find the data they are seeking. The disk continually spins while a movable access arm goes to the track where the required data are stored. Film strips are contained in clusters in canisters that rotate until the proper one is located under the read–write mechanism. The desired film strip is then removed from its canister and wrapped around a small drum, at which point it is processed as a drum. Because each is mechanically different, each has specific advantages and disadvantages. Direct access devices may be compared by speed and storage capacity. The speed of each device depends on the ability of the device to go to the data (access time) and to transmit it (transfer time), and the storage capacity is determined by the maximum number of characters each device can hold.

The three primary types of devices have the following basic characteristics:

Device	Speed	Storage Capacity
Drum	High	Low
Disk	Medium	Medium
Film strip	Low	High

The IBM 2311, the standard disk pack storage device of the 1960s, has a maximum capacity of 7.25 million characters. This capacity is composed of 10 surfaces for recording data, each with 200 usable tracks on it. Each track contains 3,625 bytes. (A byte contains one alphabetical or two numerical characters.)

The advantage of the disk pack is that it can be removed from the disk drive and a different one mounted. Also, many disk drives can be connected simultaneously with the one computer.

IBM has developed a series of disks, the 3300 series, to be used with the IBM 370, which has capacities ranging up to 400 million bytes.

The IBM 2301 magnetic drum, developed during the 1960s, has a capacity of approximately 4 million characters. It can transfer data to the central memory of the computer at the rate of 1,200,000 characters per second as compared with 156,000 characters per second with the IBM 2311 disk storage.

The IBM 2321 data cell has a capacity of 400 million bytes and a transfer rate of 55,000 characters per second.

Systems analysts often become involved in determining the precise hardware configuration for an installation. This can be a very complex question, since there are so many different models of each type of device. The systems analyst must determine the following characteristics of his company's files before recommending a particular model of direct access device:

1. The size of the file
2. The anticipated frequency of inquiry into the file
3. The volume of additions, changes, and deletions from the file
4. The anticipated growth of the file

MINI-CASE 11.1

The master record of Titan Industries contains 225 characters: 25 alphabetical and 200 numeric. Current plans are to store these records on disk packs for an IBM 2311.

How many records will fit on each track?

How many records will fit on each surface?

If the master file contains 75,000 records, how many disk packs will be required to retain the file?

The disk is rapidly becoming the dominant direct access device. Removable disk packs, mounted on several disk drives, give an installation the versatility that it requires to handle diverse data needs. The newest disks, with capacities in the hundreds of millions or possibly billions of characters, may make both the drum and the film strip obsolete. These devices have low-cost, large-capacity storage equal to the film-strip devices but with a much faster access time. Magnetic drums have a still faster access time, but, by using several access arms, the disk devices are increasing their speed. Drums, however, have much less storage capacity than the newest disks.

FILE ORGANIZATION

The frequency of inquiry into the file, the number of transactions to be processed against it, and the additions and deletions to the file usually determine the manner in which the file will be organized. Direct access devices may be organized in three ways: sequentially, indexed sequentially, and randomly (or directly).

Sequential

Sequential processing on a disk is similar to tape processing. The records are strung out on the disk in numerical order, one record after another. One advantage of this method is the efficient use of storage capacity brought about by the absence of gaps between records. Ordinarily, files are not arranged sequentially on a direct access device because it requires rewriting of the entire file to update it for changes. However, some normally tape-oriented files may be written on a direct access device to take advantage of the faster processing and access time.

Indexed Sequential

An indexed sequential file allows data to be processed either randomly or sequentially. To do this the storage within the direct access device is divided into prime storage and overflow areas. The file is originally loaded into the prime storage area in sequential order. As additions to the file occur, they are placed in their correct sequential position and the last record in that group is placed in the overflow area. An index is maintained on the disk to note the location of the records in the overflow area. Deletions to the file are flagged as they occur. On a regular basis, an indexed sequential file is reorganized by a special program that arranges the entire file in sequential order again.

Rapid access to records is accomplished through the use of indexes. Each cylinder on a disk has a track index that shows the records located on that track. When there is inquiry for a particular record on a direct access device, instead of searching through every record the computer looks up the proper address in an index.

The concept of a cylinder may be confusing. Remember that direct access devices have multiple surfaces that often can be accessed simultaneously. The IBM 2316, for instance, has 10 surfaces and 10 read/write heads. Thus 10 tracks may be read at the one time. A cylinder contains all the data that may be accessed without moving the access arms (See Fig. 11-1).

Random Processing

In random processing, the systems designer establishes a relationship between the controlling number in the file, called the key, and the address of the data in storage. The relationship can sometimes be as simple as having the numbering system for item in an inventory the same as the disk storage addresses. However, this is seldom feasible because the numbering system in most applications is either inflexible or has a particular use within the organization. For instance, social security numbers have no direct relationship to addresses on a disk.

One common method of establishing a relationship between the key and the storage address is to calculate the addresses from the key number using an algorithm program. The systems designer really does not know the storage address of a particular item, but the computer is able to keep track of every record through programs. The disadvantage to such a system is that when the program calculates addresses, it does so according to a predetermined formula, which does not provide

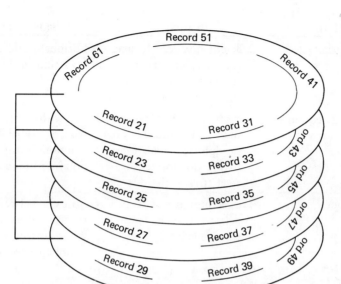

Fig. 11-1 The cylinder concept. A cylinder is a set of records that may be read with one positioning of the access arms. Since the rotating disk pack has five records on each track, and ten surfaces, the cylinder in this illustration would contain 50 records. By what method is the file organized?

for filling the storage device with complete efficiency. The gaps between records result in a less efficient use of the device's storage capacity. Figure 11-2 shows the relative advantages and disadvantages of each of the basic storage methods.

Despite their many advantages, direct access devices have some disadvantages:

cost of hardware—Rental of a drum, film strip, or disk drive costs more than rental of comparable magnetic tape equipment. Removable disk packs are more expensive than magnetic tape.

special software—These devices require special software which must be written at the installation, purchased, or rented.

personnel costs—Staffing the systems and programming areas is more expensive because the personnel to coordinate direct access systems must have higher qualifications than personnel for other storage methods.

file organization—Files are more difficult to organize. It is not unusual for a comparatively simple direct access system to take over a year to install.

File Organization Method	Advantages	Disadvantages
Sequential	Efficient use of storage capacity; faster processing time than magnetic tape files	Additions to file require rewriting entire file
Indexed sequential	Versatile, can process data sequentially or randomly; additions to file do not require rewriting entire file	Files with large numbers of additions and deletions must be re-organized regularly
Random	Large numbers of transactions can be processed efficiently	Gaps exist between data records; thus the device's storage capacity is not utilized fully

Figure 11-2

TELEPROCESSING

The potential of direct access devices is realized only in combination with teleprocessing devices. Teleprocessing is the transmission of data over telephone and telegraph lines.

Teleprocessing enables an organization to change or query the status of records from one or many remote areas. It permits handling transactions as they occur and enables the organization to maintain completely current files.

In its simplest form, a teleprocessing system would consist of a disk-oriented accounts receivable file on-line with a small computer and a typewriter terminal in the office of the company's credit manager to inquire into the billing status of any customer. The system is illustrated in Fig. 11-3.

The computer would handle inquiries typed at the terminal, finding the information on the disk file and transmitting the response back

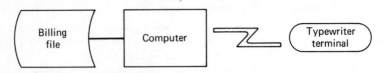

Fig. 11-3 Simple inquiry system.

to the terminal. Even in this simple system, there is much systems sophistication:

   hardware used—A company must add teleprocessing equipment, that is, a terminal and teleprocessing lines, to perform this simple inquiry. Using this equipment requires extensive training throughout the organization, because it is so different from the traditional input/output devices.

   software—Each type of remote inquiry must be programmed and most programmers are unfamiliar with this type of programming. The company must also install an operating system capable of handling messages.

It is impractical to organize a file for so simple an application. In practice the teleprocessing system would probably be similar to the one in Fig. 11-4.

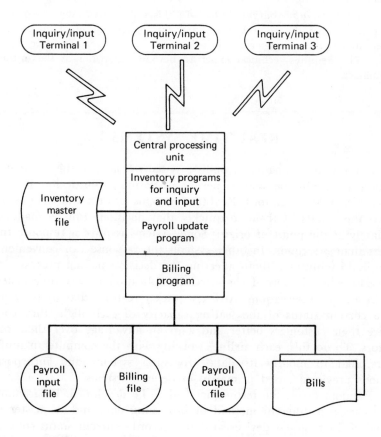

Fig. 11-4 Typical medium-sized computer configuration with an inventory file on-line and two other applications being processed.

Realistically, an inquiry network is only a part of the computer's task at an installation. Figure 11-4 illustrates several remote stations creating inquiries and input for an on-line inventory file. This system would maintain the current status on all items in the company through input from various terminals. It could then answer inquiries regarding the status of items in stock. A manufacturer who stocks many components would require these types of data in scheduling production. But this is merely a part of the information being processed by the computer. Other jobs, perhaps payroll or billing, are being done simultaneously. The configuration in Fig. 11-4 has added these complications:

multiprogramming—The central processing unit must handle several programs simultaneously. This requires both software and operations skill to allocate sufficient storage to process the required programs.

multiple input/output devices—In this system many devices are competing for use of the central processing unit. Queueing programs must be written to tell the computer the priorities set by management for computer service. This requires technical expertise beyond the realm of the ordinary programmer.

REAL-TIME SYSTEMS

The factor that distinguishes on-line systems from real-time systems is response time. On-line systems permit up-dating a file or inquiring its status from remote stations. Real-time systems process transactions and return the results of them so quickly that decisions can be made immediately at the point of origin. Some systems require a response time of less than 3 seconds. In other systems the response can conveniently come in 15 minutes without affecting the decision-making process.

The first widespread commercial application of real-time systems was in airlines reservations. Airlines quickly realized that by maintaining a current status of the seating capacity of each flight they could service their customers better and gain an advantage over their competitors. To do this, each airline, working with the computer manufacturers, had to modify its data processing systems and incorporate methods previously used primarily in defense systems.

Random access file techniques had to be developed. Programmers had to learn a different method of processing data and to master the timing of direct access devices so that a record's current status could be checked with maximum speed. Each file had to be studied closely to determine the best organizational method.

New hardware had to be integrated into the system. Buffers and message-handling equipment were developed to police the flow of transactions and inquiries coming from hundreds of locations. Terminals and communications equipment were developed to transport the volume of data required in the new systems.

Executive, or supervisor, programs had to be developed to handle the complexities of the new systems, and virtually the entire organization had to be retrained in using the new systems.

Real-time applications are becoming more numerous. For example, the New York Stock Exchange maintains a real-time system for stock prices; many bank records are maintained in a real-time environment, and factories with complex scheduling problems are installing real-time systems for their equipment usage. But real-time applications are not easily installed and require high systems sophistication.

MINI-CASE 11.2

You are the systems manager of Fly-By-Night Airlines. Fly-By-Night is a small carrier serving cities in northeastern United States and the Eastern resort areas; Cape Cod, the New Jersey shore, and the New England ski country. Most of its flights are scheduled for the nonrush hours at comparatively low rates, since many of its customers are vacationers, college students, and families. It also has a reasonably good charter business with social clubs, vacation groups, and athletic teams.

Fly-By-Night has been in financial trouble for several years. It has survived only because people like you have been able to cut overhead far below that of the competing airlines.

Three weeks ago the company hired Ed Kilmer as the marketing manager. Young and aggressive Ed was a marketing assistant for one of the larger airlines before coming to Fly-By-Night. Ed seems to have the ear of the company president, and some of the things he has been whispering into it do not make you very happy:

If we are going to put Fly-By-Night on the map, we need a classy reservation system like the big guys. A passenger comes up for a ticket . . . we give him the right one . . . we have a satisfied customer. No more showing up for a flight that doesn't exist. No more two-in-a-seat reservations. Yessir, any airline that is worth its salt has a real-time reservation system. We'll have one next year at this time or we're going under.

Right now your data processing resources consist of a tape-oriented third-generation computer, two systems analysts, and five programmers. You do the airline's accounting systems, payroll, and other statistical data. Reservations are handled through a manual system that updates seating plans at the central offices in New York through hourly telephone reports.

The president has asked you for your thoughts on installing a real-time reservation system. Explain the problem to him.

Is there any compromise possible, short of a real-time system, which could provide better information for your passengers?

• *Group Problem 11.1* •

Discuss the practicality of establishing a real-time system for each of the business situations below. List the advantages and problems associated with each situation.

The Freight Division of the Great Eastern Railroad has over 12,000 freight and refrigerator cars scattered throughout the United States. Great Eastern employs 138 people in its freight department, mostly in scheduling, billing, and maintaining an inventory on its rolling stock. The current system is manual. Bills are typed from various data supplied to the department, and scheduling is done with a large map of the United States and a fantastic collection of colored pins.

Sonomatics Corporation manufactures electronic components on a subcontract basis. It originally specialized in sonar gear components but has broadened its product line to include radar, fire-control, and communications components. Sonomatics maintains an inventory of over 300,000 parts which are assembled into more than 10,000 final products.

Sonomatics is in a highly competitive business and its management must be in a position to make accurate estimates on proposals that often require an answer within 24 hours. Larry Mahoney, the company president, feels that "We just must know whether we can do a job or not and exactly how much it is going to cost us to produce each component."

The company currently produces a weekly listing of all parts in stock on its IBM 370 Model 155. Management feels that this system is acceptable, but it would prefer more current data.

The motor vehicle bureau of Utiho, a Rocky Mountain state, maintains the automobile registry for cars in the state on a punched card file. There are currently 93,000 cars registered in the state. The file is updated monthly and a list of all vehicles registered is mailed to the regional offices of the bureau and the state police. The listing is used in identifying stolen cars, as a reference in each of the regional offices and for routine police work. The automobile bureau's computer does not currently have disk capabilities.

glossary

access time   time it takes a device to locate specific data

batch processing   system in which the transactions are accumulated and enter the computer system as a group, or batch, of input

indexed sequential   method of organizing a direct access storage device which combines some of the features of sequential and direct processing

on-line processing   system in which input/output devices have access to files through a computer

random processing   method of organizing a direct access storage device in which storage addresses are computed from the controlling numbers in a file

real-time   computerized inquiry system that provides data for immediate decisions at the source of the transmissions

transfer time   time it takes a device to transmit data once they have been located

REVIEW QUESTIONS

1. What must computer users do to utilize a computer to its full potential?

2. What developments of the 1960s led to the typical computer of the 1970s?

3. Compare the speed and storage capacity of the disk, drum, and film-strip.

4. What must a systems analyst determine before recommending a specific model of direct access device?

5. What factors determine the organization of a file?

6. Why would a company organize a disk file sequentially?

7. What are some of the disadvantages of direct access devices?

8. What software and hardware changes are required to implement an online system?

9. Distinguish between on-line and real-time processing.

10. Explain what is meant by batch processing.

11. Explain the cylinder concept.

12. How are data addresses assigned in the random processing method?

13. List five business situations in which you think a teleprocessing inquiry system would be advantageous.

14. Give three examples of where real-time systems are used in business today.

chapter 12

Data Control Methods

Objectives

More than once you have heard the story of the computer that inadvertently wrote a check for $1,000,000.00. The only thing wrong with the story is that the newspapers imply that the computer, and not the people working with it, made the mistake.

Information just does not happen to come out of the computer correctly. Data must be controlled carefully to be correct. This chapter will explain the elementary concepts and techniques for controlling computer input.

Controlling the work of a computer has many aspects. Files must be preserved from destruction and loss. Programs may be written to verify the accuracy of data. Accounting checks must be built into a system to see that no data are lost or changed. This chapter should help you understand how controls are employed to produce accurate, timely data.

TYPES OF CONTROL

One of the oldest precepts in data processing is "Never assume." Even when the source documents are perfectly designed, the keypunch operators are the best in the business, and the data center staff "has never made a mistake," one can be reasonably sure that the data reaching the computer center contains inaccuracies. Ideally, these inaccuracies are eliminated before the data affects the master file, but this is not always possible.

Errors in a data processing system are kept to a minimum through data control.

Most organizations have huge quantities of data either on its way to be processed by the computer, or being distributed after computer processing. Some data are vital to the operation of the organization and must be expedited. Other data may be processed routinely but cannot be lost along the way. Keeping track of the status of data and expediting where necessary is known as processing control.

INITIAL VERIFICATION

When data are created, they must be verified, that is, reviewed, to ensure accuracy. The two standard methods of verification are keyverification and sight verification.

Keyverification is accomplished by repeating each step of the data-creating process on a machine that checks for accuracy. When input data are created on a keypunch machine, the input cards and the source documents are brought to a keyverifying machine, where each item is keyed again. The only difference between keypunching and keyverifying is that keypunching puts holes in the cards, while keyverifying tests that the holes are in the right place. Since keyverification is a complete duplication of effort, it generally doubles the cost of creating input data. The cost is usually considered worthwhile because it is very expensive to correct errors once they are in the master file. It would not be unusual for a keypunch operator to make seven or eight errors in punching 200 cards; however, error rates of 3 to 4 percent cannot be tolerated. Keyverification will not eliminate errors. Errors will always be present in a system, but verification should reduce the error rate to tolerable proportions.

Sight verification, in its simplest form, consists of reading the information in a punched card after it has been interpreted or printed by the keypunch. The risk of not finding errors with this method is high, particularly if the data are not neatly spaced on the punched card, or it is largely numeric and contains no recognizable words, or if the volume of data are large.

A currently popular method of sight verification is to display data on a cathode ray tube as they are being punched and have the operator sightcheck it. The accuracy of this method is largely dependent upon the training and motivation of the operator.

Necessary for every phase of data input are legible, well-designed source documents. Poor source documents are a primary cause of errors in data input.

INPUT DATA CONTROL

The two basic methods of processing input data are batch and real-time processing. In batch processing, transactions are held for a predetermined period (for example, a day, a week or a month) and then processed as a group. In real-time processing, each transaction is reflected in the master file as it occurs.

Figure 12-1 illustrates the elementary control concepts in batch processing, in this case for a simple billing system. Read through the flow-chart to see how well you understand it.

The system has two phases: daily and monthly summaries. The principal reason for batching is to provide convenient subtotals to aid in error detection. In many businesses, a day's receipts would be a convenient batch. Figure 12-1 illustrates this type of company. In companies where there are thousands of transactions each day, 100 transactions might be a convenient batch.

The daily cycle provides for a control over the number of checks and the amount of dollars deposited in the bank as daily receipts. A deposit slip, listing the check numbers and amounts of each check, accompanies each deposit, and the total dollars and number of checks deposited may be obtained by add-taping the deposit slip. These two figures are the batch-control totals, whose accuracy is further assured by a verification of the deposit by the bank.

Each day, data control personnel must determine that the data entering the system in punched card form reflect the cash receipts deposited in the bank. This is accomplished by listing the day's transactions on a computer and obtaining batch totals for number of transactions and amount of receipts. When the add tape from the bank deposit balances with the control run from the computer, that batch is set aside until month end, when it will be combined with all the transactions for the month to update the master file. When the control run and add-tape

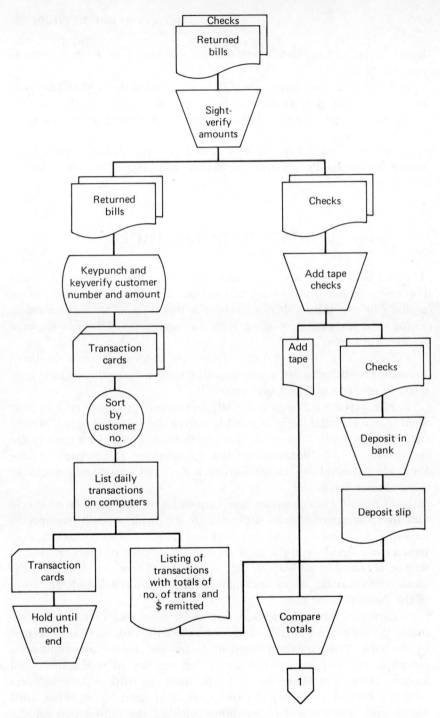

Fig. 12-1 Batch processing—a billing system.

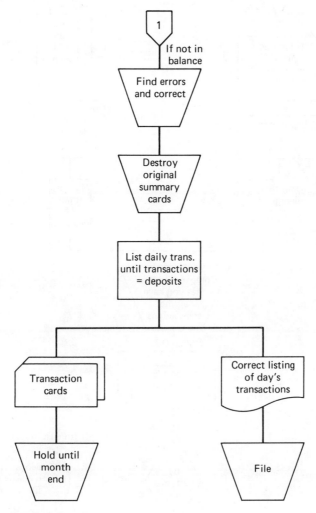

Fig. 12-1 Continued.

totals do not balance, each transaction on the control run is checked against the deposit slip until the inconsistency is found. When it is detected, and the error corrected, the control run should be done again to be sure that the error was corrected properly.

At month end, all the batches are listed together to be sure that transactions were not misplaced during the month. This run is compared with an add tape of each day's deposit-slip totals. When it is certain that all the transactions are still present, the transactions are sorted by customer number so that they can be processed against the existing master

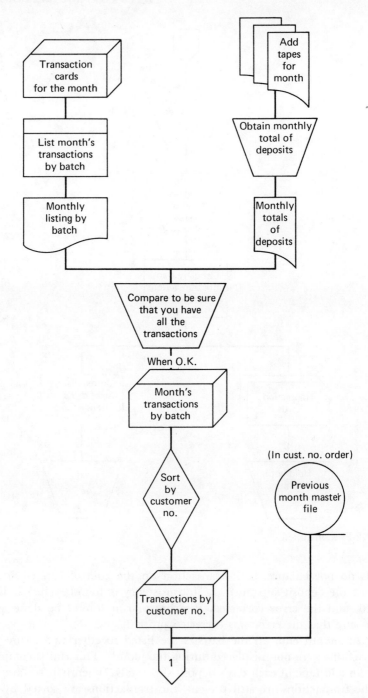

Fig. 12-1 Continued.

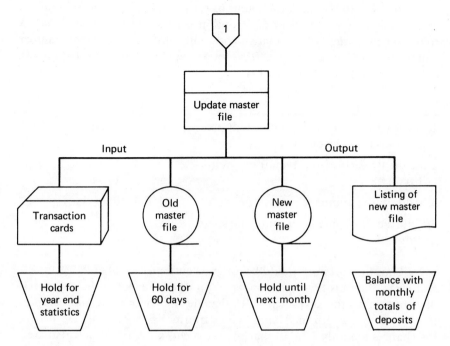

Fig. 12-1 Concluded.

file. As a by-product of the updating run, the total number of transactions and the total receipts applied to the master file are provided and are compared with the control totals previously obtained.

The controls illustrated are only some of the basic checks to be found in a billing system. Obviously, controls must be established for sales transactions as well as receipts. Moreover, the controls mentioned so far are designed only to check that the total amount of money being applied to the master file is correct; they do not verify that the transactions are being applied to the correct accounts.

Controlling the application of funds to the correct account is more difficult. A keypunch operator may have read customer number 0825 as 0325, and the keyverifier may have concurred in this error. When this occurs, customer 0825 will be overcharged on his next bill, while customer 0325 will be temporarily delighted over how little he owes. The control in this instance is when customer 0825 complains and the investigation of the source documents indicates that he is correct. Here the customers are controlling the application of money to customer accounts. At times this is adequate, but usually the adverse public relations reaction these controls incur makes their use intolerable.

One way to reduce the number of errors occurring from misreading numbers is to use the check-digit option on the keypunch machine. A computer program will calculate a check digit for each customer number before the numbers are issued. The following is a typical check-digit calculation for a seven-digit number.

Step	Example: 2473949
1. Starting from the next-to-last digit, extract every other number.	2④7③9④9
2. Multiply each of the remaining numbers by 2.	18, 18, 14, 4
3. Add up the numbers.	4 3 4 18 18 14 4 = 65
4. Subtract the units position of the sum from 10.	10 − 5 = 5

Thus the customer would be assigned customer number 2473949 − 5, and every time his account number is punched subsequently, the check-digit option on the keypunch will calculate the check digit and compare it with the predetermined one. When transposition of numbers occurs, the chances are only 1 in 10 that the same check digit will be calculated. Thus the device can detect 90 percent of the errors in punching account numbers. Insurance and credit-card companies frequently use this device.

Probably the best way of avoiding keypunch errors is to bypass the keypunching step. Scanning devices and turnaround documents substantially reduce errors in input.

GROUP CONTROL TOTALS

One system for controlling the application of money to proper accounts is illustrated in Fig. 12-2. In this system, control totals are established for blocks of account numbers. The block may be a group of 100 numbers in a small company; perhaps 1,000 in a larger company. To establish these controls, the transactions for the accounting period are run in account number order with subtotals calculated for each block of accounts and an overall total calculated for the entire file. The data being totaled are number of transactions and dollars being applied to the master file. The subtotals by block are punched into summary cards. If the overall totals balance out, that is, total dollars being applied equals dollars deposited, the summary cards of transactions by block are merged with a deck of balance-forward control cards from the previous accounting period. These

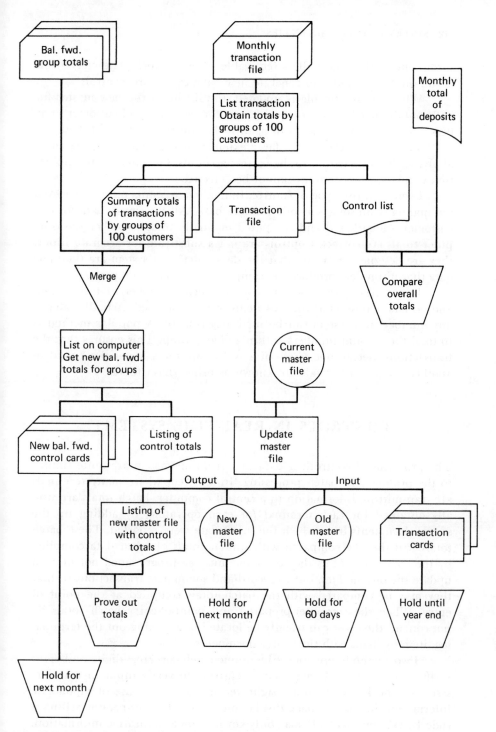

Fig. 12-2 Billing system—month-end group controls.

cards contain the total dollars receivable for each block. The merged file is run on the computer to generate new balance-forward controls.

When the master file is updated, the listing of the new master file will contain new balance-forward figures for each group of customer numbers. These will be checked out against the controls just established.

This system verifies to a large extent that the computer program is applying the transactions to the correct accounts. Of course, a misapplication within the same group cannot be detected.

Even with this type of control, individual accounts must be checked out manually on some sort of a random basis. All the source data for one customer are gathered and computed manually to see whether the computer totals are correct. Controls are not a substitute for accurate input; they are designed to ensure that the data entering a system are the same data that ultimately produce the company's information reports.

In the illustrations we arbitrarily selected number of transactions and dollars deposited as the two items to be controlled. Actually, almost any number in a system can be used as a control. A popular method is to total the account numbers within a given group. This ensures that the transactions used in one phase of a system are the same as those used in another phase. Such totals are known as using "hash totals."

CONTROLS IN REAL-TIME SYSTEMS

The problems of controlling data in a real-time system are quite similar to the problems in batch processing. In a system where many terminals are transmitting information to a central computer, batch totals are usually obtained for each terminal (or each operator), by adding up the source documents from which the input data were reported. These batch totals will then be compared with similar totals of input data compiled by the computer. Thus the computer must be programmed not only to update the on-line files, but to record and summarize transactions so that they may be compared with the batch totals compiled at the point of entry. When the computer-prepared and point-of-entry batch totals do not concur, the error can usually be located by checking out the terminal log, item by item, with the source documents.

Two methods previously mentioned, self-checking digits and sight verification on a CRT, are used extensively to verify input in real-time systems. The key to accurate sight verification is the use of alphabetic information in the feedback display on the CRT. An operator selling a code 1 ticket on flight 743 may only key in 1743 as indicative information.

However, if the CRT displays that the operator has sold a first-class ticket on flight 743 from New York to London on December 21, he should pretty well know whether he has depressed the correct keys or not. When entries are verified immediately by a knowledgeable operator who has the source data available to him, the possibility of input errors is greatly reduced.

PROGRAMMING CONTROLS

The computer programmer can do much to verify whether the data being processed by a computer are reasonable. For almost every data element, parameters may be established that will define whether the data being processed are within reasonable limits. For example, a code for the sex of an employee is normally limited to codes 1 and 2 . . . Some companies never write a check for over $500.00 . . . Other companies do not have an item number in their inventory over 5000. Each of these items can be programmed to halt a computer or write an error message when the data are outside reasonable limits. The only "mind" a computer has is the computer program; the computer does not know that it is unreasonable to write a check for $1,000,000.00, but the programmer should.

Business transactions follow patterns. The systems analyst is responsible for working with the programmers to discover these patterns and to program error conditions when transactions stray too far from these established patterns.

Similar to reasonableness checks are the consistency checks that may be programmed. A social security number always has a nine-digit number in the format NNN-NN-NNNN. Pencils are ordered by the dozen or the gross . . . automobiles are not. Error conditions must be programmed for these inconsistencies. No excuse is acceptable when the company meant to order three tractors and three dozen are delivered.

FILE SECURITY

Whether an organization's data files are stored in cards, on magnetic tape, or on a disk, there is always a danger of losing the files through fire, flood, sabotage, or error. A computer operator can mistake a vital file for a scratch tape or disk and write over it, a programmer can misunderstand the program specifications and delete records he should have updated, or an angry employee can run a magnet over a company's vital tape and direct access files. Unless a company has organized properly, the loss in such cases will be substantial and in some instances can lead to the destruction of the business.

Control of vital files is a joint responsibility among corporate management, the systems department, the operations department, and persons in the user areas. All must participate in determining the relative importance of files and how many precautions must be taken to ensure their safety.

File protection takes two forms: loss prevention and file reconstruction.

To prevent the loss of essential files, an organization usually implements a security program in its data center. Only authorized librarians are allowed access to the data library. These librarians must be trained in the data systems of the organization so that they will allow only the proper files to become available to programmers and console operators. Probably the most secure system for file preservation is for the librarian to set up each job in its entirety for the computer operators. This includes providing all input files, job instructions, and scratch files. The console operator is thus permitted to act as a check on the librarian because he knows from the program documentation precisely which files should be given to him. In addition, only authorized personnel should be allowed in the data center because strangers in a data center may be careless and destroy files accidentally.

The basic system for reconstructing files is known as the grandfather principle and is illustrated in Fig. 12-3. In an updating cycle, a file is retained until three subsequent master files have been produced, enabling a company to reconstruct a file even when both the input and output to a computer updating have been destroyed.

Some industries, such as banking and insurance, must be particularly careful in organizing their reconstruction procedures since their very business is the service these records provide. They usually have procedures that include microfilming master files regularly and storing them in remote, safe locations.

Besides files, a backup system must be provided for applications programs, computer operating systems, tables, and files not subject to changes. Ordinarily, copying these onto a backup tape and keeping this tape in a secure place will suffice.

Files updated directly do not have father or grandfather files and they are customarily copied onto a tape regularly, even daily. This process is known as a file dump. Provision must be made to retain transactions that affect direct access files to provide an audit trail when incorrect data are found in the master file. Transactions on magnetic tape may be retained for a specific length of time in the tape library. Transactions

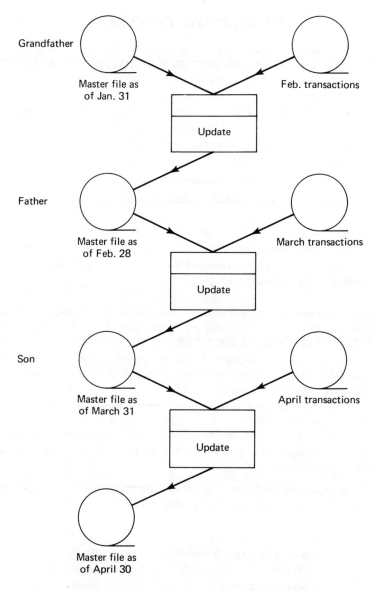

Grandfather

Master file as
of Jan. 31

Feb. transactions

Update

Father

Master file as
of Feb. 28

March transactions

Update

Son

Master file as
of March 31

April transactions

Update

Master file as
of April 30

Fig. 12-3 The grandfather principle requires that the Jan. 31
master file tape be scratched when the April 30 master
file is created. The father and grandfather are retained,
and the great-grandfather is destroyed.

entered through a terminal are usually recorded on a log at the point of
entry and the log retained for investigating problems.

WORK-FLOW CONTROL

Another aspect of the control function is expediting work and assigning priorities. Computers are normally scheduled tightly and the control group must have the entire operation under its thumb to ensure smooth work flow. For example, when it is time to run the inventory updating, the updating transactions and the existing master file must be available in the computer room. Moreover, work completed must be promptly checked and sent to the users.

MINI-CASE 12.1

The Frugal National Bank has problems with address maintenance. Frequent complaints from customers led to a survey to determine the accuracy of the addresses for customers with checking accounts. The survey indicated these problems:

1. Approximately 5 percent of the records contained inaccuracies. These included inaccurate addresses, wrong zip codes, misspelled names and addresses, and addresses with the wrong account number.

2. Common names—Jones, Smith, White, etc.—seem to be a particular problem. When Mary Jones notified Frugal National of an address change, somehow Margie Jones's address was changed.

3. Zip codes have never been put into the master record systematically. Of the sampling surveyed, 20 percent of the file has no zip code and 3 percent had incorrect zip codes. Since the bank anticipates several bulk mailings in the near future, management requires accurate zip information to take advantage of the bulk postal rates.

The customer addresses are maintained on magnetic tape in the following format as part of the master customer record:

Account Number	1– 9
Social Security Number	10–18
Name	19–40
Street Address	41–60
City	61–75
State	76–90
Zip Code	91–95
Accounting and Statistical Data	96–200

The tape is updated each day for accounting transactions. Each week, a special editing run is performed to update the name and address data in the file.

Most customers notify the bank of change of address by letter. Often, customers do not notify the bank of an address change and the bank becomes aware of the change only when the monthly statement is returned to the bank by the post office. Presently, 775 accounts are in the "address unknown" status.

The management of Frugal National is very concerned with the accuracy of this file because it feels that the customers find it hard to believe that the bank handles their money properly when it cannot get their address straight. Management wants you to make recommendations concerning the following:

1. What controls may be installed to improve the accuracy of the changes to file?

2. What can be done to correct the existing file of its current inaccuracies?

3. How can the correct zip code be put into the records for those who are missing them?

MINI-CASE 12.2

The management of the Life Protection Society of the United States is worried about the potential loss from accidental or intentional destruction of its data processing master files. Mr. Metesky, the vice-president for operations, is particularly concerned, and has formally asked the systems department for a review of the current security and reconstruction procedures. Mr. Metesky is constantly warning about the dire consequences that would accompany file destruction at the company.

"What would we do if some disgruntled employee or policyholder threw a bomb into our computer room? What if we accidentally wiped out our master file, and in attempting to reconstruct it, wiped out its backup? What if our tape librarian took a magnet and demagnetized all the backup tapes in our library? Don't tell me it costs too much for adequate protection! If we lose our files, we are out of business and someone may go to jail for negligence in handling the policyholders' money."

Certainly there is some merit in what Mr. Metesky says. If the tape files were wiped out, the company would have no idea of the premium-paying status of each of its customers. An insurance company must provide a security plan to do the following:

1. Provide reasonable safeguards against the exposure to destruction of its vital records.

2. Provide a means of reconstructing its master files even in the face of national disaster.

3. Provide the means of creating a historical record of premiums paid in case the current records are destroyed.

Life Protection has a simple accounting system for its insurance applications. It bills its customers when each premium is due, and updates its master file monthly. The transactions for each month are keypunched on punched cards and converted to tape after extensive editing and proving. The tape is then used to update the tape master file.

Provide a general plan to provide adequate security and reconstruction procedures at Life Protection.

1. Include the precautionary steps you would take to decrease the possibility of destruction of vital records.

2. What tape files would you duplicate? Which files would you retain and for how long? Where would you retain these files?

3. Would you provide printed copies of the updated files? If so, what action would you take with them to ensure the retention of vital records?

4. What action would you take to prevent the destruction of your computer programs?

glossary

data control process of verifying the accuracy of the information in a system

file dump copying a file, such as when a disk file is reproduced onto a magnetic tape

grandfather principle file retention program in which three generations of master files are held in case file reconstruction is necessary

parameter reasonable limit for an item of data

self-checking digit number generated by a formula used to increase accuracy in input data

REVIEW QUESTIONS

1. Distinguish between processing control and data control.

2. When is sight verification particularly risky?

3. How are input data controlled in real-time systems?

4. Explain how batch controls work.

5. Give examples of some of the controls that would be included in a normal payroll system.

6. Explain the relationship between well-designed source documents and input errors.

7. Explain three techniques that a company may use to ensure that cash receipts are being applied to the proper account.

8. How are hash totals used to verify data accuracy?

9. Give four examples of situations in which a program can be used to assist the control function.

10. Explain the grandfather principle.

11. What steps would you suggest to protect a company's vital records?

part V

Management
Aspects of
Data Processing

chapter 13

Project Planning and Control

Objectives

The data processing efforts of most organizations are so large and complex that they require exceptional expertise to manage and control them. This final section of the text will deal with the techniques for controlling data processing projects and the skills required to manage the data processing department.

You already know how to use a PERT chart. Now you will see how management uses this tool to evaluate progress and manage and measure the success of a systems project.

The planning, design, and installation of a system is termed a project and it is directed by a project leader, who uses the available resources to produce a new and better system for the organization.

In large companies, the installation of a computer system may take years and involve thousands of people. Planning for smaller projects also requires effective management controls to ensure the desired results. Thus project planning for any company has four main steps:

1. Organizing the resources available for the project
2. Scheduling the events in the project
3. Evaluating progress
4. Establishing standards for the project

An effective manager is essential for successful project planning. The techniques of project planning are not a substitute for good management but merely a tool to be used by managers to achieve better results. Only effective management can complete the project on time, within budget, and with satisfactory results.

ORGANIZING A PROJECT

To achieve a goal, one must have that goal clearly in mind, and thus defining the objectives is the first action taken in any project. Along with defining objectives, the corporate management must assign priorities to the various projects underway and must clarify the relationship between systems projects and existing systems. A systems project requires extensive interaction between systems personnel and people in the user areas. Users are, of course, preoccupied with their day-to-day operations and it cannot be assumed that they will be enthusiastic about participating in a systems study. Only when corporate management clearly defines the importance of user participation in systems development will the necessary cooperation exist.

To organize his project, the project leader must determine who is required for the project, when they are available, and for how long their services can be expected. The key people required in a systems project are often the key people in the day-to-day operations of an organization, and they will probably have to continue their normal routines as they participate in the systems project. In organizing their efforts, the project leader must avoid scheduling important project activities when the users are very busy with their normal duties. For users who are "always busy," plans must be made to utilize overtime, shift personnel, or add personnel to free the key systems users for participation in the project.

Important to organizing a project is ensuring that every person knows his role in the project and is aware of the corporate objectives. This is accomplished through formal training as well as informal conversations.

The project leader is solely responsible for the completion of a project, but obviously he cannot do it alone. As he organizes the project, he assigns responsibility and delegates authority for the completion of each phase of the project. Responsibilities must be precisely defined and overlapping responsibilities avoided. When a phase of a project breaks down, is behind schedule, or is over budget, the leader of a well-organized project will be able to easily identify the responsible person who can provide information and, perhaps, the solution to the problem.

Besides organizing people the project leader must budget money and order equipment, but acquainting people with their responsibilities and enabling them to discharge these responsibilities is the essence of organizing.

SCHEDULING THE EVENTS IN A PROJECT

The charting techniques discussed in Chapters 3 and 4 are the scheduling tools of the project planner. Even the simplest project should be charted so that progress can be measured. The Gantt chart is effective in simple projects, especially when the interrelationships among events are not too complex. Complicated scheduling usually requires a PERT chart.

A schedule must be flexible, because unexpected events occur that may alter materially the development of the system. Seldom do systems projects meet the original schedule at each milestone. This does not imply that schedules are made to be broken, but a schedule cannot be so rigid that when the unexpected occurs, subsequent events cannot be rescheduled.

A schedule has two primary functions: it is a plan and it is a device for measuring progress. The key steps in a schedule are called milestones, or checkpoints. As the project progresses, the date each milestone is completed is compared with the date for which it was projected. In any project, frequent progress reviews take place in which the status of events is reported and evaluated. If in the original planning stage the important milestones were anticipated correctly, reporting them completed, late, ahead of schedule, or on time has significance to the status of the project. The status of fringe events is relatively insignificant. Here the value of the PERT network as a tool for determining the relative importance of milestones is apparent.

Status of projects is often reported in terms of percentage of completion: "Activity C is 70 percent completed." As a simplified reporting device this is effective and allows easy communication with top management. The problem with percentage of completion reporting is that events on the critical path are not emphasized. A project may have 90 percent of its events complete, but if one of the incomplete events is on the critical path and is 2 years late, the project is in serious trouble.

Accurate scheduling requires extensive experience. The novice scheduler almost always does not allow enough time for activities. Even when estimates are carefully gathered, as in the preparation of a PERT network, some areas of delay are not apparent. For example, an inexperienced person may not realize that equipment or forms are often delivered late. Moreover, lead time must be provided for approvals in several areas, such as file design and input and output forms.

At the outset of the project, the project leader must determine the reporting format. Is status to be measured in days, weeks and tenths of weeks, or percentage of each job done? When are status reports to be made? Are reports to be made orally, in writing, or in chart form?

EVALUATING PROGRESS

When a project is behind schedule, corrective steps must be taken. Establishing milestones is meaningless unless the project manager can enforce adherence to schedule. Enforcement is a normal managerial duty. If a project leader cannot enforce a schedule, he should not be leading the project. If one area is consistently behind schedule, or over budget, the project leader must discuss the problem with the individual responsible and take corrective action. A variety of options are open to the project leader:

Increase the budget

Increase manpower in the form of overtime or additional people

Add equipment

Change priorities

Replace the individual responsible

The project leader must determine the real cause for unsatisfactory progress. Perhaps it is a budgetary or personnel problem. Too often a major cause of apparently unsatisfactory performance is that the original schedule estimates were wrong, and therefore progress is as good as can be expected under the circumstances.

Projects have many target dates but few deadlines, and the project leader must distinguish one from the other. When target dates are missed, there may be some grumbling, but missed deadlines result in financial loss to the organization.

At the outset of a project, the project leader should not allow himself to be pressured into committing himself to unreasonable target dates or deadlines. Unreasonable deadlines are costly because unnecessary effort is put forth to meet them. Moreover, failing to meet them often creates morale problems.

The project leader must remember that his is not the only project under way and that delays will routinely occur simply because another, more important, project may have to be tested before his. Schedules are highly dependent upon priorities and should be planned accordingly.

ESTABLISHING STANDARDS

Initially, the project leader must establish the objectives of each phase of the project. Each phase must be of a controllable size and every task within the phase spelled out. The project leader and the individual responsible for the phase must agree upon the human skills and other resources required to accomplish each task. They must also agree on the expected outputs from these tasks. Ultimately they must decide upon the measurable outputs expected from each phase, particularly since this output will usually be the input to the next phase. It is these measurable outputs that will be examined throughout the project to evaluate progress.

For each phase of a project, the status of time to complete tasks, personnel utilization, and unforeseen problems should be reported to the project leader. This report is then reviewed by the project leader and the managers concerned to evaluate progress. Also evaluated is the quality of work, as reflected in the outputs from each phase. This periodic review has four main tasks:

1. To review project progress
2. To analyze the impact of delays on the entire project
3. To examine any problems existing in the quality of the data
4. To anticipate developing problems

PROJECT MODIFICATIONS

For a variety of reasons, changes must sometimes be made in a project while it is under way. Requests for changes must be evaluated carefully, according to several criteria:

1. The impact on the present schedule
2. The impact on the resources available for the project
3. The cost
4. The effect on the deadlines for the system

Poor planning is often the cause for changes to existing projects, and has several other consequences as well:

obsolescence—The systems in an organization tend to become obsolete quickly.

poor follow-up—The responsibility for follow-up falls upon corporate executives instead of project leaders.

inflexibility—Systems become inflexible, so that minor modifications result in extensive program writing.

lack of documentation—Procedure writing and documentation are, in general, neglected.

• GROUP PROBLEM 13.1 •

The Thomas J. Hawk Company, manufacturer of TommyHawk Toys, hired you last year as a systems analyst. TommyHawk currently has a data processing staff of three systems analysts and seven programmers. The company has had an IBM System/3 card system for 3 years and several weeks ago it ordered a 360/30 with a disk-operating system. The new system will have four tape drives, two disk drives, a reader-punch, and a high-speed printer.

All the current programs are written in RPG II. The program library includes 120 programs for the following applications:

> Inventory, reported monthly
> Payroll
> Customer billing
> Miscellaneous accounting procedures

TommyHawk's management has selected you to coordinate the transition to the new system. It has specified the following for the new system:

1. The standard programming language will be COBOL. Eventually all the existing programs will be rewritten.

2. The hardware is to be installed 10 months from today.

3. All technical training is to be done at the computer manufacturer's schools.

4. The primary systems change will be a conversion to a daily inventory system. Management has established an 18-month target date for this project.

5. Management expects a reasonable cost saving in clerical operations as a result of this conversion.

Management expects a preliminary report on how you expect to organize the project. Include the following items in this report:

> List of anticipated problems
> Suggested staffing

Training plans
Schedule of events, including a conversion schedule
Milestones through which you expect to measure progress

You realize that your task is loaded with pitfalls, primarily because of all the unanswered questions. Prepare a report that will give management a realistic view of the impending conversion.

glossary

deadline   scheduled date, which, if not met, will be costly to the company
project   planning, design, and implementation of a system
target date   date on which a certain event is expected to be completed

Review Questions

1. What can the project leader do about getting key people, who are "always busy," to participate in a project?

2. What is meant by the statement: "Project management deals mainly with people"?

3. What constitutes unsatisfactory progress on a project?

4. What are two purposes for a schedule?

5. When is percentage of completion an adequate reporting technique?

6. What alternatives are available to project leaders when progress is unsatisfactory?

7. What should be accomplished in the periodic reviews of project status?

8. What criteria should be used for evaluating proposed changes?

9. What steps are normally included in project planning?

10. What tools are available for measuring progress in a project?

11. How rigid do you think a project schedule should be?

12. Distinguish between a target date and a deadline.

13. How are standards for project evaluation arrived at?

chapter 14

Managing the Systems and Data Processing Areas

Objectives

Different companies have adopted various ways for organizing their data processing effort. However, wherever computer systems are installed, certain specific functions must be carried out. Among them are systems planning and design, computer operations, programming, data control, and user participation. This chapter explains these functions and how they must interact to produce successful systems.

Training personnel is often talked about, but more often, neglected. You will become familiar with the training requirements of each type of data processing professional along with the needs of the systems users and corporate management.

MANAGING THE SYSTEMS AREA

The systems department is usually engaged in many activities simultaneously. To cope with this, systems departments usually organize themselves into project teams, each headed by a project leader. Thus the organization within a systems department will often be quite fluid: a junior analyst may find himself one month reporting to the project leader of a team that is designing a new payroll system, then joining a group studying the feasibility of renting optical scanners for the next 2 months. Organizationally, systems departments must be flexible.

Logically, managers seek flexible people to be systems analysts. Technical knowledge is important in systems analysis, but the pure technician does not necessarily make the best systems analyst. Ideally, technical ability is combined with common sense and an attitude of accepting and creating change.

Managing a systems department requires additional ability. Systems analysts are constantly involved with problems in every area of the business. The state of the art in computer technology is constantly changing. Installing new computer systems has traditionally been characterized by long hours, traumatic experiences, opposition, and frustration. Thus coordinating the loose ends of a systems department requires unique skill.

Managers are often evaluated by their ability to anticipate future change. The systems manager must be aware of developing changes not only in his field, but of those taking place in his company and business in general. Today, the role of management information systems goes well beyond performing routine accounting functions. Information systems include such diversified areas as sales analysis and projections; marketing plans; design techniques for manufacturing; routing transportation; queue analysis for retailing; analysis of scheduling and machine utilization in production, and many more applications.

The systems managers of the 1970s must cope with several complex problems:

1. Obsolescence of techniques
2. A general tendency to decentralize the data processing function
3. Less control over data in a period when data are becoming more vital to the organization
4. The introduction of the user as a participant in systems development

Systems managers must live with change, not only in the systems of the organization, but in the very way systems and data processing is being performed.

POLICIES IN THE SYSTEMS AREA

The systems manager is responsible for developing the policies necessary to promote an environment in which new systems may be introduced. The policies cover a wide variety of problems:

1. Methods of developing new systems jointly between the data processing and user areas

2. Definition of career paths within the systems area

3. Mechanism for resolving disputes

4. Use of facilities; this includes the use of the computer by programmers for test time, and the use of remote terminals by users, programmers, and systems analysts

5. File integrity, including the preservation of data in the data library and the availability of live data to programmers for testing

6. Priorities in job scheduling

7. Maintenance of procedures and programs

8. Interrelationship among the various components of the data processing area

DATA PROCESSING AREA

The composition of the data processing area varies with the size and the nature of an organization's business. In smaller organizations, the data processing area is relatively simple, usually consisting of an operations department and a systems/programming department. As organizations grow larger, the data processing organization becomes more complex.

Organization specialists debate what is the best location in a company for a data processing group. Originally, the data processing department usually came under the Controller since the original data processing applications were in automating the accounting process. As the role of data processing broadened to provide information for the entire organization, the data processing department tended to become an independent function. Since the work of the data processing function in most companies today transcends departmental lines, the Data Processing Director must have enough influence in the organization to effect changes that will satisfy the information needs of the entire organization. Figure 14-1 illustrates a "normal" data processing organization. The structure is by no means universal; organizations vary widely in size and relative importance of data processing. As a general rule, data processing is of greater importance in companies that perform services, such as banks and insurance companies, than it is in manufacturing companies.

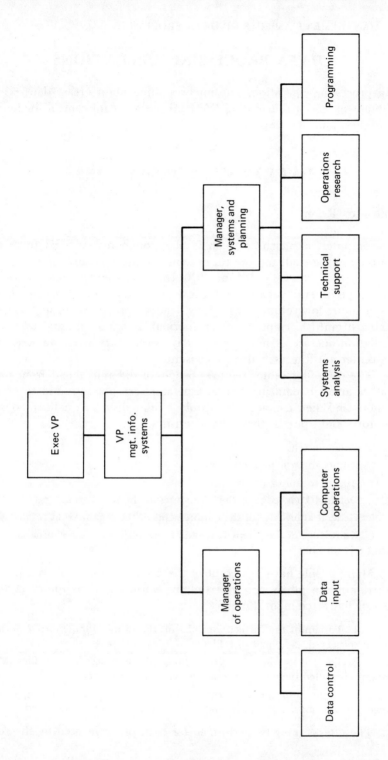

Figure 14-1

233

DATA PROCESSING OPERATIONS

Data processing operations encompasses three main areas: data center computer operations, including EAM processing; data control, including the library; and data input.

DATA CENTER OPERATIONS

Computer Room

The computer, or machine room is now commonly referred to as the data center. We shall use the three terms interchangeably.

A typical data center of the 1970s consists of at least one computer, with its peripheral devices, and EAM equipment for preparing input data or doing low-volume jobs. Many data are processed through remote terminals; multishift operations are normal. It is not unusual to see an installation operate 24 hours/day, 7 days/week. Interaction between the data center and the user areas is constant.

The computer center requires people of different talent from those in other areas in data processing. Operators are not required to be innovators, and their contact with people is limited, but a qualified console operator should possess these characteristics:

Common sense

Ability to anticipate problems

Ability to follow procedures

Detailed knowledge of the procedures at the installation

General knowledge of the requirements of the organization

Knowledge of the peculiarities and characteristics of the equipment with which he is working

Many people have a concept of the computer operator as a button pusher, but the job is not that simple. Normally, a computer console operator has three main duties:

1. To mount the correct data files on the proper input/output devices. This includes card, tape, and disk files.

2. To activate the appropriate program for processing the files. Most programs are called in from a program library on a disk pack.

3. To monitor the typewriter console for programmed messages. The console operator must take appropriate action when trouble is indicated.

These tasks must be performed for each program used by the computer. In today's multiprogramming environment, the console operator must shepherd many programs through the computer simultaneously. When an employer is looking for a console operator, he wants someone who can calmly follow instructions and act with sound judgment when things go wrong.

Data control methods were discussed in Chapter 12. Data control is not only the concern of the data processing area; this function is often decentralized. The goal of data control, however, is universal: accurate data disseminated on time.

Data control is responsible for the master files of an organization and has four primary objectives:

1. Screening data for reasonableness before it affects the master files

2. Determining the accuracy of the master file after transactions have been applied to it

3. Physical maintenance of the data library

4. Coordinating input gathering and output dissemination.

Data Library

Today, an organization's vital records are contained in its card, tape, or disk library. Even when the source data for creating files is retained, the cost of reconstructing an entire file is considerable when it is lost or destroyed. Ordinarily, the data library has a fireproof safe in which vital records are stored and access to this safe is restricted to two or three people. When all of a company's vital records are available in one place and can be easily destroyed by fire or a magnet, it is encumbent upon the data processing area to provide adequate measures to ensure the integrity of these files.

The librarian's job goes beyond the preservation of vital records. The library must provide the data center with the files that it requires for daily operation. The console operator is responsible for mounting the correct tape for a job, but the librarian must see to it that the correct tape is available to him. The coordinator between these two functions is the control group, which has the responsibility for bringing together the various data requirements of the data processing area. It may control a batch of transactions from the receiving department through keypunch and see to it that this input is available to the console operator when the inventory master file is to be updated. Computers rent for hundreds of dollars per hour; it is costly to keep them waiting, and even more costly when management must wait for data for decision making. Control must coordinate efforts and avoid such delays.

DATA INPUT

Computer input is created locally at the computer installation and remotely at other terminals. The problem in both cases is to provide accurate input.

The keypunch room is a primary data source at many installations. Whether the data are on punched cards or tape, the problems in keypunch installations are similar. A serious input problem for management is to provide the environment in which the staff wants to work. Keypunching can be very boring, and bored employees are inaccurate. The data processing management must motivate keypunch operators in several ways:

1. By emphasizing their importance to the entire organization. The company often does not survive without data input; and inaccurate input is costly.

2. By providing adequate surroundings for the keypunch staff. Clean, well-lighted space is a necessity. A carpet on the floor to lessen the noise and provide status is not unreasonable.

3. By rotating work assignments; most good key operators thrive on learning new jobs. This temporarily slows down production, but in the long run, better morale and increased versatility lead to higher production.

Remote generation of input has its unique problems; for example, how does one get 500 clerks in 500 locations to care that the input data they create are accurate? This is largely a question of overall corporate morale, but the data processing area must provide the controls to improve accuracy. Audit trails must be established to identify errors. The individual who causes the error and the pattern of errors that occur must be identified. This type of data may be provided by requiring every operator to key in his code number as he takes over a remote terminal. The computer can be programmed to store transactions by individual and provide a record of each person who is creating input for the system.

DATA CENTER MANAGER

A data center manager's primary responsibility is for the efficient operation of the data center while providing acceptable service to management and the user areas. He normally reports to the Director of Data Processing. Many companies have been negligent in selecting data center managers: too often the senior console operator is automatically chosen as the manager of the data center. This policy acknowledges that experience in data processing operations is important, but too often senior operators lack the other qualifications for being successful as a data center manager. These qualifications include:

1. Ability to synthesize the needs of the data center staff with the corporate objectives
2. Acceptance of change
3. Current technical knowledge
4. Broad corporate knowledge
5. Ability to represent management to the staff, and staff to management

The responsibilities of a data center manager are similar to managers in other aspects of business:

1. Formulating operations policy within the framework of corporate policy
2. Acting as liaison with the other data processing areas and the users
3. Establishing training procedures
4. Establishing standards of performance
5. Acquiring and developing staff
6. Budgeting
7. Actively participating in systems development and maintenance
8. Maintaining high morale

BUDGETING THE RESOURCES OF THE DATA PROCESSING AREA

A data processing area possesses these resources:

1. People and their collective skills
2. Equipment
3. Physical facilities, such as office space
4. Financial resources—money that has been allocated for a given period
5. Time

People are the most crucial resource available. The data processing manager must continually develop the skills of the personnel already in his organization and must hire people with new skills. Almost every systems project requires a blend of skills, and only a skillful manager can find the right combinations to bring about the desired systems results. Data processing skill is rare and cannot be squandered on nonproductive projects.

The data processing manager must determine the relative importance of systems development and current production within his organization. Programmers feel that they never get enough time to test programs. Operations people feel that interruptions from the programming staff slow down normal production. The data processing manager must maintain a proper balance.

Moreover, a proper balance must be maintained among the various departments as to how much money each is allowed to spend. The ultimate consideration for each decision is how the allocation of each amount of money will lead to profitability in the organization.

The systems, programming, and operations departments share a common goal: together they must satisfy the information needs of the entire organization. To achieve their corporate goals, these departments must continually engage in a free exchange of knowledge: the systems people must be aware of the problems the operations department faces in the data center, and the data center personnel must be cooperative in dealing with systems people. A new system is not installed effectively unless all departments within the data processing area have mutual respect and sufficient rapport.

DATA PROCESSING AND THE USER AREAS

The data processing and user areas have mutual goals: each must cooperate in producing better systems that will lead to corporate profitability. The attitude of the systems analyst toward the user is important. The user is an expert within his own area, and the systems analyst will never thoroughly comprehend the problems in the user areas unless he is informed of them by user personnel. Equally important, however, is that the user acquire a working knowledge of the data processing function. Most users are quite anxious to learn more about the computer. Both systems analysts and users must participate equally in a free exchange of information.

Errors in a system are inevitable, and those which occur in any system are a source of friction between the systems and user personnel. All effort should thus be concentrated on reducing the number of errors rather than assigning blame to avoid as much as possible such nonproductive friction.

TRAINING RESPONSIBILITIES OF
THE SYSTEMS DEPARTMENT

Training is one of the major responsibilities of the systems department, yet it is often put aside because other needs are more apparent. The training requirements of the Systems Department fall into three categories:

1. Management training
2. Training data processing professionals
3. Training the systems users

Management Training

Having its management knowledgeable in data processing is perhaps the most important training goal of a systems department, yet management training in data processing is often totally neglected. The corporate managers are ultimately responsible for a company's systems, so it is reasonable that they be provided with the knowledge to properly discharge this responsibility.

What must a manager, such as a marketing manager, a treasurer, or the executive vice president of a firm know about data processing? Most managers certainly do not need to know computer programming, but a manager must know how to use the computer as a business tool that can help him perform his job better. Thus management training has two aspects: to provide information appropriate for managers and to develop attitudes suitable for maximizing the use of the computer.

Developing a training program for managers is difficult for several reasons. It is hard to get a group of managers together at one time for a training session. The traditional problem is that a "busy executive" has more important things to do than "learn about computers." Developing instructors to teach EDP to managers is difficult also. Many very good technical teachers lack the managerial attitudes necessary to be effective with executives. Very often the task of training managers has been delegated to the computer manufacturers. This, too, has its problems: a computer manufacturer quite naturally will emphasize the potential of the computer and may be a little lax in specifying the problems and limitations associated with it. The systems department should coordinate the data processing training for the company's managers and include the following program:

1. Survey of computer systems fundamentals
2. Review of computer potential and computer limitations
3. Review of the current state of computer use at the manager's company
4. Analysis of how the computer is used as a business tool, especially in closely related businesses
5. Analysis of the impact of the computer on the business organization in general, and on the manager's particular business

6. Participation by the managers in various aspects of systems development

This type of training program only partially lends itself to formal classroom presentation. It requires full participation by the managers and a willingness on their part to modify their business concepts in light of computer technology. The key to successful management training in data processing is the environment in which the training is conducted. This environment must be created by both the managers and the data processing professionals.

A management training program in data processing never ends because the field is changing so rapidly and because a certain amount of turnover is normal among managers. In many companies in which the managers are well trained in computer concepts, the continuing program consists largely of exchanges of information in informal conversations and of keeping up with current developments through trade publications. No large company today can afford to have a management that lacks fundamental data processing knowledge or whose data processing concepts are obsolete.

Training the Data Processing Professional

Data processing professionals are usually classified into five categories:

Key machine operator
Data control specialist
Machine operator
Programmer
Systems analyst

The positions, however, are often not clearly defined and extensive overlapping of duties exist: some systems analysts program, some programmers also operate equipment. The training program for data processing professionals must be tailored to meet the needs of each company. However, guidelines for a training program may be formulated.

Key machine operators must acquire three skills: speed, accuracy, and procedural knowledge. Training key machine operators is a constant problem, because there is often heavy personnel turnover in these positions.

The primary objective in training key machine operators should be to increase accuracy. Once in a system, mistakes are costly to detect and reverse. When key machine operators are thoroughly familiar with the procedures in a certain system, their accuracy increases. The systems department and the supervisor of operations are responsible for providing the operator with this knowledge. Formal, well-written procedures help, but they are effective only when the job is already thoroughly learned and they are used for occasional reference. When the operator is learning a job, informal training sessions, with plenty of questions and answers and trial and error, are required. In general, the supervisor of operations is responsible for training new operators in existing systems and the systems department is responsible for training the key machine group, including the supervisor of operations, in new and developing systems.

Data control specialists require a detailed knowledge of the procedures associated with a system and a working knowledge of computers. The systems department should provide both formal and informal training to satisfy these needs.

Machine operators have traditionally been trained by the "sink-or-swim" method. Very simply, the operator was given the job and was quickly told how to do it. He was given some procedures, often out of date, and was expected to do the job. If he failed, someone else was hired who could swim in this environment. Computer console operators must be thoroughly trained to perform their jobs correctly, and this requires the following:

1. Orientation in the company's policies and goals

2. Explanation of the policies and goals of the data processing function

3. Survey of computer systems fundamentals

4. Introduction to the company's hardware, including actual operation of the equipment

5. Brief course in the job control language used at the installation

6. Demonstrations in the use of the software packages available

7. Review of the procedures of the data center

The common technique of on-the-job training (OJT) is sometimes supplemented by technical courses provided by computer manufacturers. The primary objective for training is to have the operators acquire a detailed knowledge of the workings of the computer and of the procedures in the computer center.

Systems analysts usually are either experienced programmers who have demonstrated an ability to do systems work, or college graduates who have the potential and desire to do this type of work. Each type must be trained differently, yet the objectives of the training program for both would be to learn the following:

1. Systems techniques

2. Computer technology

3. Existing systems in the company
4. Effective techniques for good relations with coworkers

These objectives can be achieved by several means: courses in colleges and universities, in-house training programs, courses conducted by computer manufacturers, professional seminars, and training programs conducted by professional consultants.

The systems techniques that a systems analyst must master are those discussed throughout this text, including charting, problem solving, and data gathering and analysis.

Computer technology includes a knowledge of programming, an understanding of computer operating systems, a knowledge of the hardware currently available, and some clear ideas on the state of the art. in systems analysis. These are best learned at manufacturer's schools or at seminars conducted by various societies associated with the data processing industry.

The existing systems within an organization are learned through in-house training. Seminars are useful when a group of systems analysts will be working on the same application. Systems analysts who must learn a particular system are best taught through conversations with people who are currently expert in that system. The effectiveness of this method is largely dependent upon how good the systems analyst is at "brain picking" and how well motivated the experts are in sharing their knowledge with the systems analyst. It all comes down to just how well the systems department is accepted by the corporation.

The most difficult aspect of training systems analysts is that of improving their ability to work with others, because the goal is not to increase knowledge but to develop attitudes. The systems analyst must realize that to be effective he must convince many people, particularly the systems users, to share information with him. It is equally important that the users have confidence in the systems the analyst produces. The systems analyst derives his authority in an organization from the systems users' acceptance of him as a producer of effective systems. To gain this confidence the analyst must have extensive technical knowledge plus an ability to exchange ideas with people. In most organizations, the latter characteristic is more important and most frequently lacking.

Programmers are trained originally at a college, a programming training school, or a computer manufacturer. Unfortunately, in many organizations training programmers is a hit-or-miss proposition after the initial schooling. One course for training a programmer in-house would include the following:

1. The high-level language used at the installation (for example, COBOL, FORTRAN, PL/1, RPG)

2. Computer systems fundamentals

3. Company's policies and goals

4. Systems and programming standards at the installation

5. Another programming language, a low-level language, in the case of a potentially good programmer

6. Basic systems-analysis techniques

7. Advanced programming techniques

8. Relationship of programming and operating systems

Most programmers will not make good systems analysts because the two positions require differing talents and attitudes. Good programmers are solution-oriented—they solve problems that are presented to them; systems analysts are problem-oriented—they consider apparent and real problems to define precisely the problems facing an organization.

Training the Systems Users

A chronic business complaint is that the people using a new system are often the last ones to know how to use the system. When this accusation is true, the fault almost always lies with the systems department.

Obviously, when a new system is being introduced the systems department must spend much time training the people who will use the system. But if the systems department waits until conversion to a new system is imminent before it implements its training program, it is probably too late.

Training user personnel is a continual process, and its effectiveness is less dependent upon the systems department's ability to teach than upon the department's creation of an atmosphere in which change is accepted. The systems department has a perpetual problem in gaining acceptance in an organization, because to many people the systems department represents the computer, a threat to their existence in an organization. To have people accept its suggestions for better systems, the systems department must convince the systems users that its proposals are not a threat to them personally and that the proposals will be helpful to the entire organization.

Thus there are five objectives for training user personnel:

1. To develop an attitude of cooperation between the systems department and the user areas

2. To explain the details of proposed systems changes to the entire user staff

3. To cultivate the attitude that each area should strive for the corporate good

4. To provide the users with a working knowledge of EDP

5. To give the users an idea of the impact of impending systems on the organization and on their particular area

These objectives are noble, but difficult to accomplish. To achieve them, the systems department must involve the users in its work.

The ideal way to train user personnel is to have them participate in the development of the system. When the system is fully designed, the users must feel that it is "our system," not "their system," and this attitude can develop only when they are instrumental in designing the new system. Thus user personnel should be part of the feasibility and systems design teams, they should have a good deal to say about the conversion process, and they should have the final say as to when the system is ready to be converted.

Because of turnover, users have a continual problem in training new personnel. Training new people in existing systems is primarily the responsibility of the user area, but the systems department can provide substantial assistance.

ALLOCATION OF SPACE

The systems area is often confronted with unique space-allocation problems. Systems analysts feel that they require a private office because of the nature of their work, and programmers need privacy to concentrate. Allocating space involves not only providing for realistic business needs, but also for the privacy and status requirements of the data processing workers.

One necessity in office space for systems development is a conference room where meetings, interviews, and data analysis can take place. Its only requirements are that it is reasonably comfortable, private, near the systems department, and reasonably near a supply of coffee. It must be a pleasant room in which to work and think.

The operations department has very unique space requirements: computer areas must be free from the perils of unauthorized visitors, yet accessible to many people; the floor of the computer room is usually raised between 8 to 12 inches to hide the cables that connect the various devices; operators need adequate space in which to work; and, in a batched processing environment the data input area should be near the computer area. Figure 14-2 illustrates a layout for a typical data center.

MINI-CASE 14.1

Upright Furniture has been manufacturing furnishings for the home for over 50 years. The company has stressed its manufacturing excellence while neglecting to update its office procedures, with the result that they have become inefficient. Upright now has a new and aggressive management which is determined to improve office procedures. Management has committed itself to a substantial budget for automating the company's inventory, accounting, and management-information procedures. Included in these plans is the ordering of an IBM System/3 disk-oriented computer with delivery scheduled for October of next year.

Currently, there is no perpetual inventory system at the company. The accounting records are all maintained manually. Management decisions are based generally upon outdated information or the business intuition of top management. Within the next 2 years, all this is expected to change.

You are the manager (and the only staff member) of the new data processing department. One of your primary concerns is to staff your department. You have budgeted for the following people for next year:

Systems analyst A	Jan. 15
Programmers A and B	Mar. 1
Systems analyst B	Mar. 1
Programmers C and D	July 1
Keypunch operators A and B	Aug. 1
Console operator	Sept. 1
Data control specialist	Sept. 1
Keypunch operators C and D	Oct. 1

The installation will use COBOL as its primary programming language.

You intend to hire one experienced systems analyst and one experienced programmer. The rest of the staff is to be selected from qualified people in the company, if they are available, or from new personnel.

Design a training program for your staff. Display the schedule for this training program on a Gantt chart.

What training would you provide for the management and users within the organization?

MINI-CASE 14.2

LaFemina Fashion Shoppes has just hired you as the director of data processing. In your interviews with Linda LaFemina, the company president, it was apparent that the company's data processing systems are in

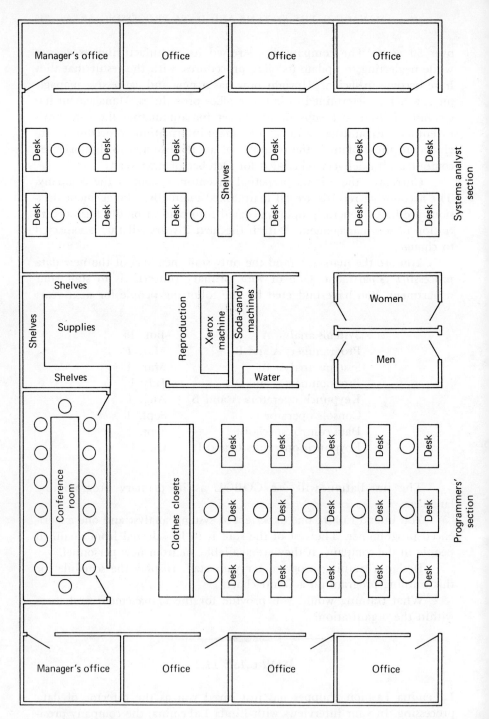

Fig. 14-2 Typical data processing organization.

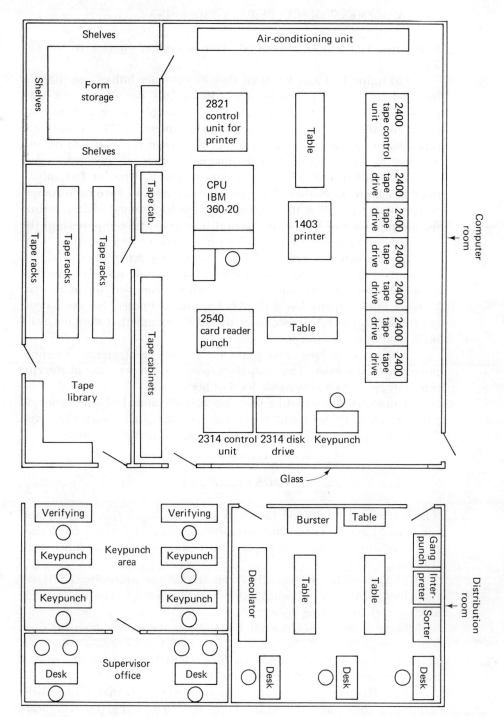

Fig. 14-2   Continued.

247

bad shape. You will be the fourth data processing director in the last 6 years.

LaFemina Fashions has been slow in customer billing ever since it installed its computer 7 years ago. "We simply cannot get our sales people to work with the various systems we keep putting in here" Ms. LaFemina told you during an employment interview. "Computers are supposed to save money, but so far they have been very costly to us, and our systems are no better than the manual systems we used years ago."

Your initial feeling is that the data processing effort at LaFemina's has never been emphasized. Your predecessors seem to have been competent computer people with little management background and no feeling for the problems of the ladies' apparel industry. The computer and the rest of the company existed as two separate camps.

The human resources in the data processing department consist of one systems analyst, three programmers, one console operator, and six keypunch operators. No one has been with the company for more than 2 years. The company has a third-generation computer, but its systems are similar to the EAM systems of the 1950s, except that they use magnetic tape instead of cards.

There are no long-range plans for systems development. Training programs do not exist. The company expects you to get some of the current systems up to a reasonable level of operation.

You think you will like your job at LaFemina Fashions. The job pays exceptionally well and is obviously challenging. Prepare a memo for Ms. LaFemina outlining your plans for the immediate future.

MINI-CASE 14.3

The McFarland Publishing Company publishes a full line of hard- and soft-covered books, along with several magazines. McFarland has had a computer installed for several years, with some success and much frustration.

McFarland has successfully computerized the processing of its address files, with only the usual number of problems. It also has a workable payroll and billing system.

Many of the managers at McFarland complain a lot about the computer's performance. They had read of some of the wonders computers perform, so they really cannot see how McFarland's computer cannot always make a simple address correction.

Bud Metheny, the executive vice-president, feels that management training in the computer area has been neglected totally. To complicate matters, the executive offices of McFarland are located in midtown New York while the computer center is located at the plant, 30 miles away, in New Jersey. Most of the executives have not even seen the computer, nor do they really know the director of the computer center. Joe Ahearn, the center director, has been with the company only 6 months and has been busy with the routine problems of adjusting to a new environment.

Mr. Metheny has asked you to organize a program to train the executives. His objective is to increase their knowledge of computer potential and limitations so that the organization may avail itself better of this expensive and potentially profitable tool. Mr. Metheny has arranged to reserve, for a 2-month period, 1 hour per week of the time of any (or all) of the corporation's executives to carry out whatever program that you propose.

Write for Mr. Metheny an outline of your training plan.

---

glossary

OJT   on-the-job training

REVIEW QUESTIONS

1. What characteristics should a console operator possess?

2. What are some of the resources that a data processing area must possess?

3. What are the responsibilities of a console operator?

4. What are the responsibilities of a data center manager?

5. What prerequisites must a potential data center manager possess?

6. What can be done to motivate the people who produce computer input?

7. What items should be covered in the policies of the systems area?

8. What should be the goals of a management training program in data processing?

9. What should a training program for console operators include?

10. What should a data processing training program for managers include?

chapter **15**

Practical Development of a System

Objectives

In this chapter you will see how each aspect of systems development was handled at a fictitious company, Valve and Leake Plumbing Distributors. Valve and Leake is typical of many companies who are encountering for the first time the need for data processing. Examine each phase in their systems development and determine where you agree with their actions and where you would have done something else.

INSTALLING A COMPUTER AT VALVE AND LEAKE

The Valve and Leake Corporation is a wholesale distributor of plumbing and heating equipment located in the greater Boston area. Its main office is in Quincy, Massachusetts, and it has warehouse and distribution facilities in Brockton, Marlboro, Salem, East Boston, Concord, and Quincy, Massachusetts.

Until 2 years ago the organization was composed of six independent wholesalers who consolidated to share each other's expertise, facilities, and inventory. Originally, each branch was a family-owned, self-sustaining business. In consolidating, the new company, Valve and Leake, secured additional capital for expansion through a public sale of stock.

However, much of the past remains in Valve and Leake. Despite the consolidation, each location operates virtually independently of the others as a self-sufficient profit center. Each has its own accounting, inventory, and billing system, and all systems are manual.

The central management of Valve and Leake at the Quincy office is composed of highly professional businessmen with years of experience in plumbing distribution. Each branch has competent management, staff, and salesmen, all with a thorough knowledge of the plumbing business. No one in the organization is familiar with EDP.

Marvin J. Leake, the company president, realizes that there is tremendous potential to be realized by consolidating some of the company's functions. For instance, inventory items, such as bathtubs in various colors, are kept in stock at every branch, even though each branch could share the other's inventory. The problem is that it is currently impossible to keep up-to-date inventory records without excessive clerical costs. A periodic inventory is conducted annually at each branch. This takes over 3 months to itemize and evaluate, as each branch has over 9000 parts in stock.

Customer billing is costly at Valve and Leake. All invoices are prepared manually, including price lookup and extension. To ensure accuracy, an extensive manual verification of price procedure has been installed at each branch.

Each branch purchases independently since it alone knows what it has on hand and what its customers need. Mr. Leake wants to:

1. Centralize billing of all branches through the Quincy office
2. Establish and maintain a perpetual inventory of items
3. Centralize purchasing

To accomplish these objectives, Mr. Leake feels that the company must install a computer. He is ready to make the move but he realizes that the company lacks data processing expertise. Mr. Leake hired an office manager, Dexter Franklin, for the Quincy headquarters largely because Mr. Franklin knows data processing equipment and systems. He has asked Mr. Franklin to help organize the company so that data processing equipment may be employed successfully.

Mr. Franklin read the company prospectus. Several facts caught his eye. The company has sales in excess of $7,000,000.00 per year and showed a gross profit last year of $560,000. Most of the company's assets are tied up in the $2.1 million parts inventory it maintains. The company employs 104 people: 36 clerical, 14 management, 6 sales, and 48 in stock maintenance.

Valve and Leake is a fictitious company, but its problems are real. How would you begin if you were Dexter Franklin?

Below is a chronology of events showing one course of action for Valve and Leake.

October 1

The systems request at Valve and Leake seems direct and simple. The company president wishes to install a computer. But beyond that nothing is defined. Mr. Franklin's task is to convert this directive into a workable document so that everyone concerned will understand the project.

Franklin wants to ensure management involvement in the systems development. After talking with Mr. Leake and all the branch managers, he convinced Mr. Leake to issue the following memo.

```
TO:    All Officers and Managers
FROM:  M. J. Leake
DATE:  October 15, 19--
RE:    Systems Review Committee
```

Effective immediately, those named below will constitute the Systems Review Committee. The purpose of this committee is to make preliminary recommendations as to the feasibility of installing EDP equipment in Valve and Leake. The committee:

```
Chairman    Max Kaufman—Vice-President
Member      Jim Chambers—Manager, Brockton
Member      Elgin Bradley—Manager, East Boston
Member      Dexter Franklin—Manager, Quincy
```

November 15

Dexter Franklin visited each branch to find out more details about the company's operation. The Systems Review Committee met three times and agreed not only that installing a computer in Valve and Leake was feasible but that the present would be a particularly good time to install one. The committee made these opinions known to Mr. Leake and decided to document their findings in the form of systems requirements.

Besides internal use, the systems requirements could be used by computer hardware and software sales representatives in forming proposals for Valve and Leake. The document, which in effect is a formalized systems request, is shown below.

SYSTEMS REQUIREMENTS FOR VALVE AND LEAKE PLUMBING DISTRIBUTORS

Valve and Leake Plumbing Distributors is a wholesale distributor of plumbing and heating equipment. Valve and Leake has its main office in Quincy, Massachusetts, and has warehouses and distribution facilities in Brockton, Marlboro, Salem, East Boston, Concord, and Quincy, Massachusetts.

Current Data Processing Systems

Each location currently operates independently of each other. All systems are manual. Periodic inventories of stock are conducted annually or when otherwise required.

Systems Requirements

Valve and Leake plans to install a data processing system that will provide:

1. Current inventory status at each branch
2. Timely and accurate customer billing
3. Control of purchases and accounts payable
4. Centralization of the accounting function in one location

Objectives for the Proposed System

1. Substantial reduction in the ratio of inventory to annual sales
2. Freeing of key people from clerical operations
3. Improved cash flow through more rapid billing and improved follow-up on overdue accounts
4. Greatly improved management information in the areas of:
   a. Sales analysis
   b. Reduction of redundancies in inventory items among the branches

    c. Analysis of contribution to profit of individual inventory items

    d. Analysis of each location as a profit center

    e. Availability of stock to service customer's needs, including inventory sharing among the branches

    f. Reduction in cost of clerical operations

Valve and Leake feels that any new system must provide the following:

    1. Immediate access to an on-line inventory file. Inquiries are projected at approximately 200 per day.

    2. Weekly customer billing.

    3. Weekly analysis of and computerized followup on overdue accounts receivable.

    4. Regular accounts payable analysis and computerized checkwriting.

    5. Ability to update all files through terminal input.

    6. Daily analysis of sales volume.

Specific Systems Problems at Valve and Leake

    1. Input data are created at six remote locations.

    2. The organization has had no experience in electronic data processing.

    3. Servicing customers requires immediate response to customer needs.

    4. Various billing methods are required for different types of customers.

Volume Data

Master file data:

Items in inventory among all the branches	15,000
Customers	2,500
Suppliers	1,100

Transaction data:

Sales	5,100 invoices per month
	8 lines per invoice
Payables	1,250 orders per month
	6 lines per purchase order

Conclusion

Dexter Franklin is authorized to initiate a feasibility study to develop a plan to achieve the objectives listed above.

If you were Dexter Franklin, what steps would you take next?

January 1

Dexter Franklin initiated the feasibility study by developing a plan. His memo documenting this plan is shown below.

```
TO:   Marvin J. Leake
FROM: Dexter Franklin
DATE: Jan. 10, 19--
RE:   Plan for Feasibility Study
```

At the outset of this project, I wish to outline my intentions for developing a plan for installing a data processing system at Valve and Leake.

Objective of the Study:
    To provide a plan for installing a data processing system to meet the corporate objectives set forth in the systems requirements.

Scope of the Study:
    The study will include every major aspect of the company's operations, including billing, inventory, and purchasing. It will coordinate these functions for all six branches.

Schedule of Events:
    1. Interviewing and data gathering at all branches
    2. Development of preliminary plan   Feb. 15
    3. Management review   Feb. 20
    4. Further data gathering and refinement of plan
    5. Feasibility report   Mar. 10
    The study will require my full attention for the next 2 months plus the availability of key people at each branch on a regular basis.

January 25, 19—

Dexter Franklin spent most of the next month gathering information for the feasibility study. He learned and flowcharted the current procedures at each location. He became acquainted with almost every worker in the organization and earned their respect and cooperation. On February 25 he reported his preliminary findings to Mr. Leake, the Systems Review Committee, and the operations managers of each branch. Many problems and misunderstandings were ironed out and many of Dexter's questions were answered.

Dexter also talked with sales representatives and systems analysts from four of the leading computer manufacturers as well as representatives from three software support companies to bring himself up to date on the state of the computer arts. After another month of study and fact gathering, he submitted the following feasibility report.

Based on your knowledge of data processing, what recommendations do you expect in Dexter Franklin's report?

FEASIBILITY REPORT FOR VALVE AND LEAKE PLUMBING DISTRIBUTORS

March 14, 19——

Systems Summary

After studying the alternatives, I recommend that Valve and Leake install a computer at its Quincy headquarters. The proposed system would require a central processing unit, a punched card reader, and a low-speed printer at the main office, and input/output typewriter terminals at each of the six distribution centers. The system will require 10 million bytes of disk storage and a teleprocessing capacity to handle data input and inquiries from six remote stations. The CPU will probably require 16K bytes of storage to handle the programs to be used in the system. This type of configuration is available from several computer manufacturers.

When the system is fully installed, there will be three master files: the billing master, the inventory master, and the accounts payable master. Each file will be updated at the end of each working day through transactions transmitted daily from each location. The transactions will be proved before updating. The status of each file will never be more than 24 hours old, which we feel is sufficient for this type of business. Invoices will be prepared daily and a billing statement mailed weekly to all customers. The flowcharts in the Appendix display the proposed system in more detail.

Cost Expectations

Although we have not yet selected specific vendors, the following summary itemizes the approximate cost of the proposed system.

Hardware rental	$2,500–4,000 per month
Telephone-line connections	800–1,100 per month
*Additional professional personnel	1,000–1,500 per month
Additional management time for new system	2,000 per month
Miscellaneous costs	400 per month

---

* This does not include the cost of training the personnel currently on hand to work with the new system.

There will be an initial setup cost—to establish a computer center, buy disks, and get the system underway—of approximately $3,000.

This preliminary analysis indicates an annual investment in the proposed system of a minimum of $54,000 and a maximum of almost $82,000.

Expected Benefits

There are currently 15 people in the organization who are directly involved in the billing operation. The new system will require no more than 10. Assuming an average salary of $7,000 per year, this represents a savings of $35,000 per year in direct salaries.

The company is in the process of growing and its growth will be limited without the potential that a computer provides.

The proposed system provides management with the ability to control and reduce inventory. This would free large amounts of capital for investment in more profitable areas.

Personnel Requirements

1. Assignment of a top management executive to be responsible, among his other duties, for the computer installation.

2. A manager/systems analyst to solve the day-to-day managerial problems of the computer center. He should be someone already in the organization and must be strongly committed to the success of the corporation and the computer center.

3. A full-time computer programmer/systems analyst to program all applications and work with the manager/systems analyst in designing systems in full detail.

4. Between three and five control specialists, skilled in clerical data processing, who know Valve and Leake's current operations well. Their function will be to work in the computer center as problem solvers and to ensure the accuracy of invoices, bills, remittances, purchase orders, and receipt of delivery.

5. Data input specialists at each location. The new system will require one person at each location to key in data concerning sales, deliveries, purchases, and remittances. People currently in the organization can be trained for these positions.

Training Requirements

The organization requires extensive training in three areas: management, technical staff, and clerical staff. Although a more detailed training program will be spelled out in a subsequent report, I must emphasize here the importance of having the key people in our organization participate fully in the systems development and in the formal training sessions.

A program will be established in which all managers and corporate executives will be expected to participate. We will arrange technical training for our programmer and backup programmers with the computer manufacturer from whom we rent the equipment. The clerical staff will be trained on the job as the system develops.

Problems To Be Solved During Systems Design

1. A uniform billing structure for all branches must be clearly defined.
2. Precise hardware specifications must be determined.
3. Management information requirements must be defined in writing.
4. Forms design must be finalized.
5. Files must be designed in full detail.
6. Programming specifications must be written.

Conversion Plan

As much as possible, the billing system should be centralized before the computer arrives. This would assist in training the data center personnel and develop uniformity in billing throughout the organization.

We should concentrate on installing the billing system first and have it ready for operation before the computer arrives. When the computer is installed, two locations, East Boston and Brockton, should be converted immediately to the new system. Each month, one more location should be converted to the new system, so that 4 months after the computer is installed, all locations will have been converted to the new billing system. We anticipate that the old and new systems should run in parallel for 1 month at each location.

We expect to convert the payables system within 2 months after the billing system is installed in each location since that system will be more simple than the billing system. When both the billing and payable systems are working well, approximately 8 months after the arrival of the computer, the inventory maintenance system should be implemented.

Review Questions

1. Dexter Franklin's proposed system uses transaction pending files which are checked out before updating instead of directly updating the master files. What advantages do these files have? What disadvantages? Which way would you use to update these files?

2. Examine the controls implied in the flowchart. Explain how Dexter Franklin plans to create accurate input.

3. Do you feel that this feasibility study would be a sufficient plan from which to design a system? What other material would you include in the feasibility study?

4. Do you feel that the systems design and conversion schedules are reasonable? What changes would you suggest?

April 1

The feasibility report was approved by Mr. Leake and the Systems Review Committee. Dexter Franklin was appointed project manager for the design and conversion stages.

January 1

The billing system was installed 1 month late. Programming bugs still existed, but the bills were going out correctly.

November 1

The inventory system was installed several months late but is operating adequately. Dexter Franklin estimates that it will take 6 months to clear up the routine problems that exist in the system.

December 15

Dexter Franklin was appointed data processing director at Valve and Leake. Mr. Leake has asked him to coordinate the corporate efforts for the new and larger computer that it anticipates ordering next month. (See the Appendix for a chart of the proposed system.)

Appendix

Flowcharts of the Proposed
System at Valve and Leake

SYSTEMS DESIGN SCHEDULE

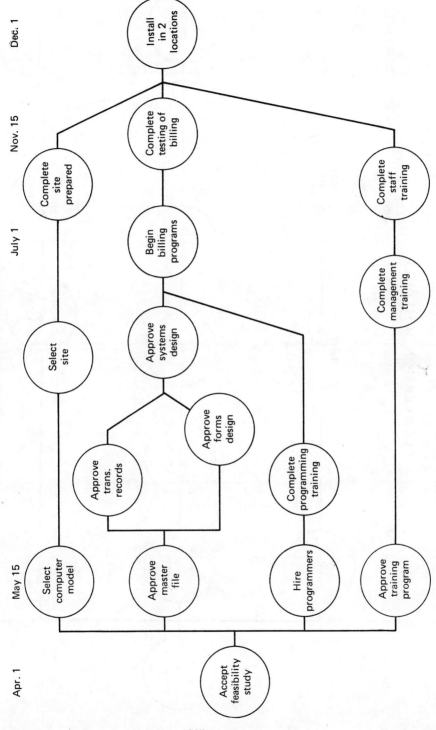

CONVERSION SCHEDULE

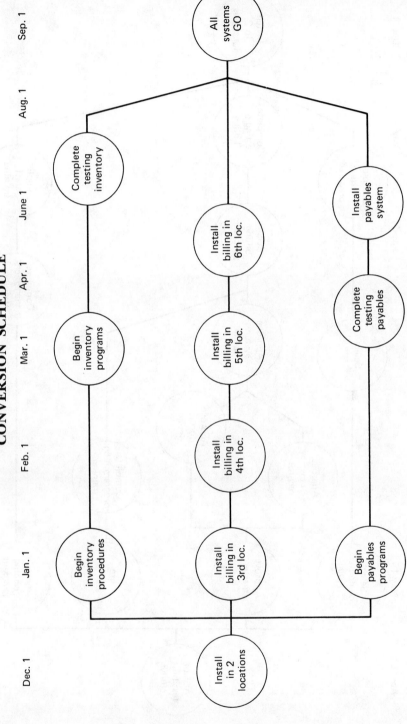

PRELIMINARY SYSTEMS DESIGN
DAILY SALES PROCEDURE

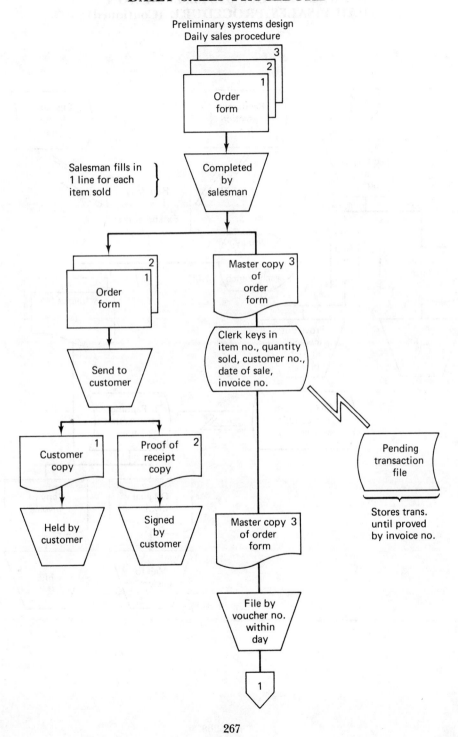

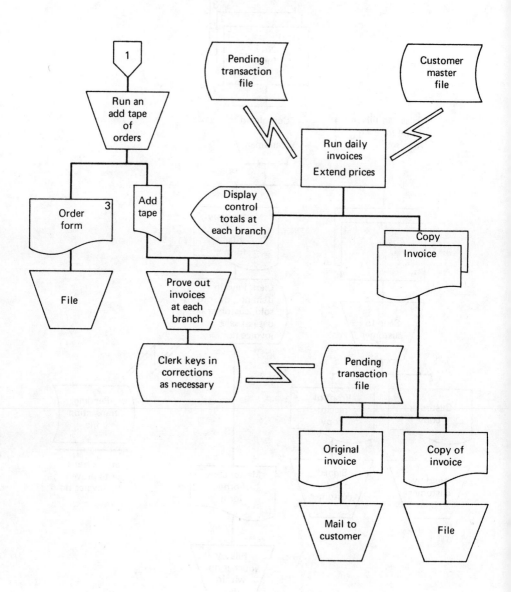

CASH RECEIPTS PROCEDURE

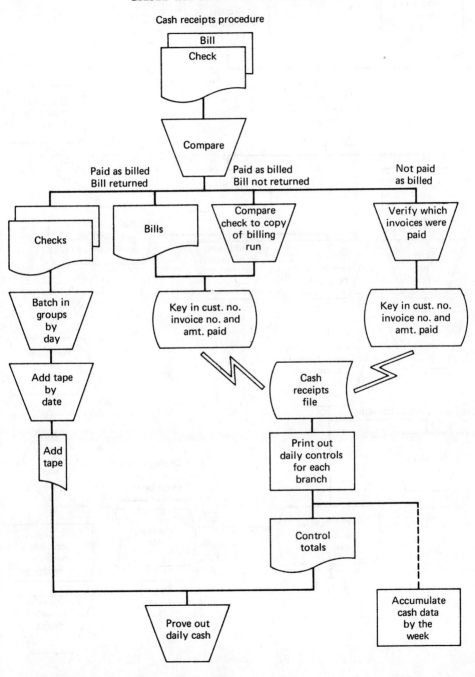

Cash receipts procedure

Bill
Check

Compare

Paid as billed
Bill returned

Paid as billed
Bill not returned

Not paid
as billed

Checks

Bills

Compare
check to copy
of billing
run

Verify which
invoices were
paid

Batch in
groups
by
day

Key in cust. no.
invoice no. and
amt. paid

Key in cust. no.
invoice no. and
amt. paid

Add tape
by
date

Cash
receipts
file

Add
tape

Print out
daily controls
for each
branch

Control
totals

Prove out
daily cash

Accumulate
cash data
by the
week

ACCOUNTS PAYABLE—DAILY

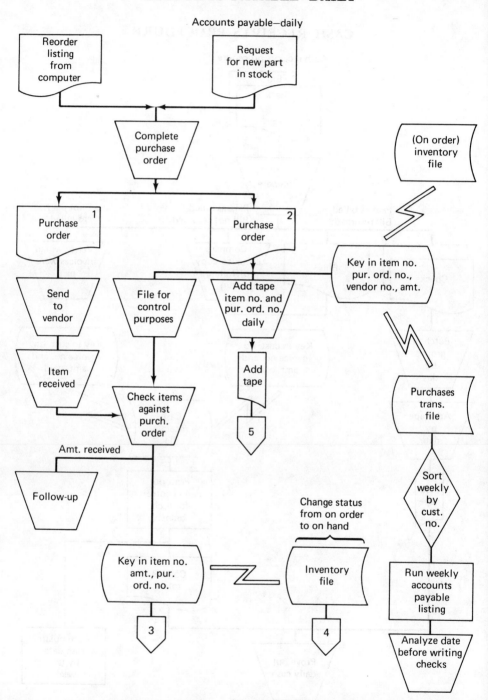

Accounts payable—daily

Reorder listing from computer

Request for new part in stock

Complete purchase order

Purchase order 1

Purchase order 2

Key in item no. pur. ord. no., vendor no., amt.

(On order) inventory file

Send to vendor

File for control purposes

Add tape item no. and pur. ord. no. daily

Item received

Check items against purch. order

Add tape

5

Amt. received

Follow-up

Purchases trans. file

Sort weekly by cust. no.

Change status from on order to on hand

Key in item no. amt., pur. ord. no.

Inventory file

Run weekly accounts payable listing

3

4

Analyze date before writing checks

ACCOUNTS PAYABLE—DAILY (Continued)

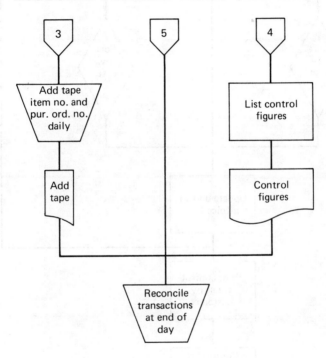

ACCOUNTS PAYABLE—DAILY (Continued)

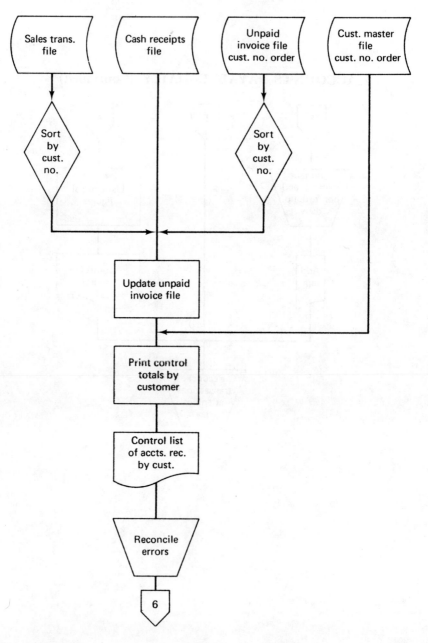

ACCOUNTS PAYABLE—DAILY (Concluded)

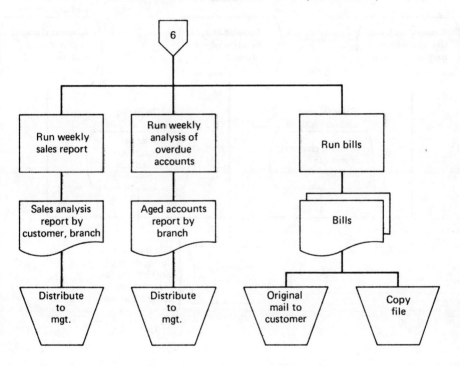

INVENTORY PROCEDURE—DAILY

Inventory procedure—daily

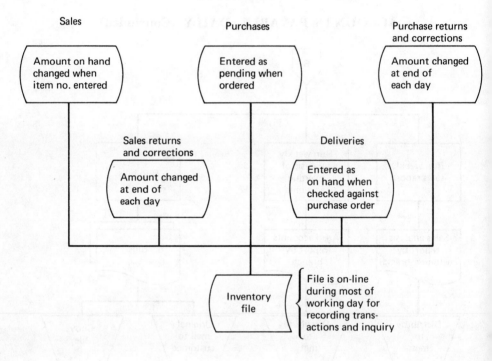

Index

Index

A

B

C